IT'S A DUCK.
AND IT'S DEAD!

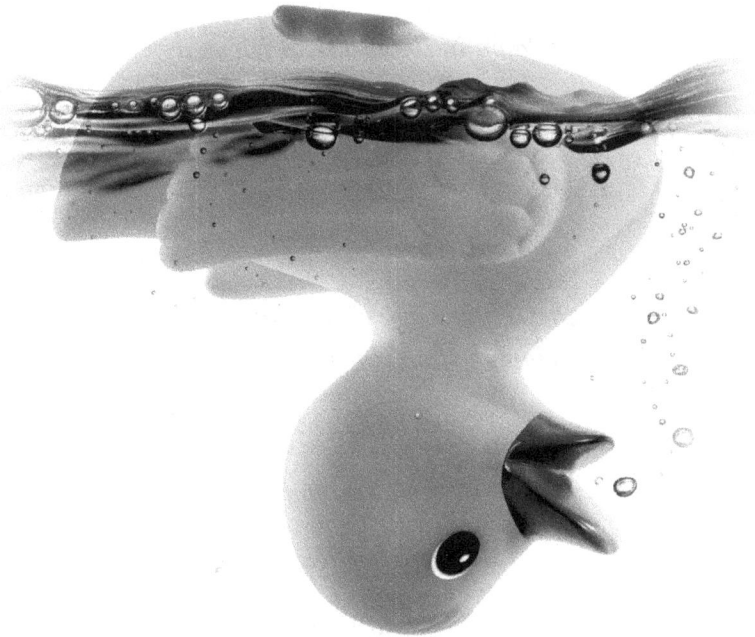

Also by Maralys Wills

Wait for the Wind

*Revenge of the Jilted Draperies
and Other Sweet-and-Sour Stories*

*So You're Seventy ... So What?
How to Love the Years You Thought You'd Hate*

The Tail on my Mother's Kite: A Memoir

*Buy a Trumpet and Blow Your Own Horn:
Turning Books into Bucks*

*Damn the Rejections, Full Speed Ahead:
The Bumpy Road to Getting Published*

A Clown in the Trunk: A Memoir

A Circus Without Elephants: A Memoir

Save My Son

Scatterpath: A Thriller

*Higher Than Eagles: The Tragedy and
Triumph of an American Family*

Fun Games for Great Parties

Soar and Surrender

A Match for Always

Mountain Spell

Tempest and Tenderness

Manbirds: Hang Gliders & Hang Gliding

It's a Duck. And It's Dead!

A Trail of Adventure Through Six Generations

Maralys Wills

Lemon Lane Press · Santa Ana, California

Book Designed by Sue Campbell Book Design

Lemon Lane Press
1811 Beverly Glen Drive
Santa Ana, CA 92705

To contact the author: maralys@cox.net
www.maralys.com

Contents

Acknowledgements 7

Prologue 9

Chapter One: Swept Away by a Sea Puss................................11

Chapter Two: It All Began at a Jolly-Up...............................21

Chapter Three: Misled by Grantly Dick-Read.......................29

Chapter Four: "Chub" Develops a Battering Ram..................35

Chapter Five: A Different Kind of Kid.................................41

Chapter Six: Daredevils in Montclair....................................47

Chapter Seven: The Inscrutable Patriarch.............................51

Chapter Eight: Random House and Beyond..........................57

Chapter Nine: Moot Court Daze..63

Chapter Ten: The Rotten Apple Syndrome 69

Chapter Eleven: A Mixed Bag at Winnetka 75

Chapter Twelve: Orange County, Here we Come 81

Chapter Thirteen: Moving Like An Inchworm 87

Chapter Fourteen: A Frenetic Stolen Summer........................91

Chapter Fifteen: The Shopworn Shoebox.............................93

Chapter Sixteen: The Two Doctors Klumpp..........................97

Chapter Seventeen: The Sports Bonanza...............................105

Chapter Eighteen: Tragedy Brings a Reunion.......................111

Chapter Nineteen: Nerds to the Rescue 113

Chapter Twenty: The Sleepless Sleepover..............................119

Chapter Twenty-One: We Lost a Prince.................................125

Chapter Twenty-Two: The Aftermath....................................131

Chapter Twenty-Three: A Classroom Beckons Again 141

Chapter Twenty-Four: Serious Enough for the Mayo Clinic.............147

Chapter Twenty-Five: Aloha, Art and Ruth...........................151

Chapter Twenty-Six: The Anti-Choke Squad.........................155

Chapter Twenty-Seven: The Next Generation Adds New Luster........159

Chapter Twenty-Eight: At Last ... A Boy! 169

Chapter Twenty-Nine: A Trio of Virginia Belles 173

Chapter Thirty: The Drama Runs Both Ways 181

Chapter Thirty-One: A Second Goodbye.. 185

Chapter Thirty-Two: Bravo, Match. Paul... 191

Chapter Thirty-Three: A Long Life's Big Reward.............................. 195

Chapter Thirty-Four: Five Pixies at a Distance 201

Chapter Thirty-Five: Why We're Hanging On.................................... 207

About the Author... 209

Acknowledgements

As always, no project as large and complicated as a book is produced entirely by one person. But in this case my gratitude goes first to my husband, Rob, for contributing, almost single-handedly, one of its standout features—the chapter titles. Rob is particularly good at this ... able to grasp concepts and lend drama at the speed of light. He's also an unfailing resource as I grasp for "just the right word" or phrase. Over the years he's given me some great book titles, too.

A warm thanks to our granddaughter, Christy, who spent months digging up stories on various sides of the family. To this end she made countless phone calls, read ancient documents, and dug around in old family archives. The stories on my two grandfathers and my father's German background are largely because of her. And she did it simply because she wanted to, creating richly detailed booklets on the long-ago families from whom we all came. The current generations are her beneficiaries.

As with all my dozen recent books, my critique group has been there consistently, offering insights where they're most needed. I never consider a chapter finalized until they've seen it. Plus they're all great writers themselves, which makes our sessions both vital and fascinating, like going to the movies. So thanks to Barbara, Allene, Pam, P.J., and Terry.

In the end, a book is only as good as how it looks and how it's put together. For this I can thank Sue Campbell, who has been the genius behind my best-looking covers and a whiz at doing the final, expertise-required jobs ... getting it ready to be brought out in print or ebooks. She's also endlessly patient. A hearty thanks to Sue.

Last, but not least, I want to thank my kids, grandkids, and great grandkids—for being such interesting people that my writing a book about them was almost inevitable.

The author and husband, Rob.

Prologue

IN SPITE OF OUR 69 YEARS OF MARRIAGE, MY HUSBAND, ROB, AND I do not consider ourselves *old*. As always, late mornings find Rob drowning out all conversation with the shrill grinding of his orange juicer. Rendered momentarily silent, I'm wondering how I could possibly be out of vitamins—since I just filled the 7-day container three days ago. Happily for Rob, his juicer prevents my saying once more the banal words I'm thinking: *Time sure flies when you're older.*

From then on, as I prepare brunch, I'm the rubber band between the stove and his family room chair. Eventually, breakfast around here is like eating at a library, with both of us reading, but Rob also watching the Dow Jones averages.

Which wouldn't do for dinner ... meaning a choice between staid, high-end restaurants or, more often, joining casual folks at eateries like KFC, McDonald's, Costco, and In 'n Out.

Meanwhile, we both still drive and we travel often to foreign countries; Rob makes stock trades and writes essays, and I teach a weekly class in Novel Writing.

Yet our immediate family has now grown to 41 members, among which are a flock of great grandchildren. Lucky for us, several families still live close enough so we can call each other last minute: "What are you doing for dinner? Grab the kids and let's go to Ruby's!"

The following story is about our great-granddaughter, Nora, who has never been ordinary. I swear, she was born talking, and if she didn't actually say it, she could have told the Delivery nurse, "You've got spots on your uniform."

One day, at about age four, Nora and her brother, six, were spending some time with our nearby daughter, Tracy. At the moment Tracy's husband was out of town, but her teenage son, Dane, was there, busy mowing the lawn.

Next door a family of ducks had settled into the neighbor's pool. Tracy took Dane and the kids over to see what nature had wrought. But then the neighbor's dog caught one of the ducklings and maimed it with puncture holes.

Dane rescued the small, struggling swimmer and held it close until it died. The two younger kids were devastated.

Soon afterwards, Tracy was talking to her husband, Brad, long distance. In her inimitable way, Nora demanded, "Let me talk to Brad." So Tracy put her on. Quickly sizing up the situation—that no adult would stay long on the phone with a child—Nora went right to the point. She said, "It's a duck. And it's dead!" With that, she surrendered the phone.

Grandma Maralys gets photobombed by great-granddaughter, Annalise. Though Nora was the original pronouncer of deceased waterfowl, forthright boldness is a strong trait of all the cousins!

Behind her back, Tracy and Dane tried to control their laughter.

FOR ROB AND ME, NORA represents the spirit of the clan this saga describes.

CHAPTER ONE

Swept Away by a Sea Puss

SINCE I WAS TEN YEARS OLD, I'VE BEEN TRYING TO SAVE MY OWN LIFE.

At around nine, when I first began reading "grown-up" magazines like *The Reader's Digest*, I abruptly learned that human beings were essentially disposable. It seemed from those pages that any number of missteps could carry you away—which is how I developed an internal ferocity aimed at keeping my grip tightly connected to earth.

My younger brother, Allan, and I mostly grew up on a lushly forested, 320-acre ranch near Mt. Shasta, California. Because Mother was rich and raised us carelessly, Allan and I languished in and about the ranch house, with more free time than our poorer neighbors.

"We can't play today," the mile-away Deetz boys often told us, "we've got to help Dad with haying. He loads the truck and we smash it down." If it wasn't haying that kept them shackled, they had laundry to hang or cows to milk.

Thus forced, especially in summer, to spend extra time with books and magazines, I happened to read early on that the killer, lockjaw, was prevalent in farm settings, especially around rusty nails. To my horror, the news was awful; first the nail penetrated your foot (to what depth they didn't say), then your jaw tightened, and soon you died. Since our ranch was a virtual garden of semi-buried rusty nails, I began fearing that I might somehow step on one and fall prey to this dread affliction. Before long, I was secretly measuring the opening of my mouth, using my thumb joint as a kind of ruler.

Though the route to my tonsils never narrowed, the *Digest* kept me alert and perpetually wary. It seemed there were always new, fearsome possibilities—from a patient riding in a hospital elevator and suddenly unable to breathe (saved only because a doctor happened to be riding with him) ... to the youths who came down with paralytic polio.

For whatever reason, my beloved magazine was never short on stories about fatal diseases, thus casting over my pre-teen years a great many moments of bright, stark panic. But I kept them to myself, suspecting I'd never be taken seriously ... or worse, people would laugh.

Of course my otherwise-engaged mother never knew.

Actually for a couple of summers, local kids did succumb to polio, mostly from swimming in our nearby Abrahms Lake ... ensuring my private vow that I'd stay miles away.

Eventually I recognized a lifelong truth: you can read too much ... and consequently it's possible to consume too many of life's precious hours worrying.

STRANGELY, IT NEVER OCCURRED TO ME THE ONE DAY I WAS IN actual danger that I might not make it to sunset.

As happened so often during my growing-up years, our mother regularly pawned off Allan and me for temporary raising by others. She was beautiful and sexy, and though I scarcely noticed at the time, too much of her attention was focused on her own concerns—a struggling guest ranch and her third marriage, this time with a wonderfully handsome man. Hans was a Swiss ski instructor she'd found abroad, and she was deeply in love.

I do remember her enthusiasm as she asked one day at the start of summer, "Maralys, wouldn't you like to go visit your father on Long Island?"

"Well ... yes. Maybe I would." Which is strange, because I was twelve at the time and hadn't seen "Ted," as we children called him, since he'd come to our ranch when I was ten and visited Allan and me for seven glorious days. For that brief span we'd had his full attention, and yes, unlimited kindness—this from a father we hadn't seen since babyhood.

My heartbreak after his departure lasted for weeks. Each morning when I awoke my first aching thought was, *Ted isn't here anymore, Oh, God, how will I stand it? How can I survive without him?*

Now something inside stood guard over my emotions. A brief hesitation. "I'll go, Mom. Will you take me there?"

"Oh, no, honey," she said. "You'll go by train."

I stared at her. "By myself?"

She smiled. "How else?"

TALK ABOUT FEAR. THOSE FIVE DAYS CROSSING THE COUNTRY ALONE demonstrated the invisible bond between mind and stomach. Unaware that I was beyond tense and deep into fright, I wondered only why I suddenly felt so sick. For those five days my stomach rebelled. A sour taste entered my mouth and the very thought of food turned me away. Though I went often to the dining car, most of the food remained on the table.

Yet the minute Ted met me at the station, all symptoms disappeared. Suddenly back to my normal self, I became part of his second family … with his new wife, Virginia (also my mother's name), and their four children.

It was perhaps a week later that Ted and his sister, Margaret (like my father, a doctor), and her husband Art took us all to Jones Beach … but first to Ted's small cottage. Every detail of that day remains vividly in memory.

Besides his family, Ted had brought with us a doctor friend, a flabby man who, at lunch on the patio had made me uneasy. Nay, more than uneasy—he gave me the creeps. His fingers seemed to be constantly on the prowl, accidentally brushing over parts of my body. Very soon it seemed not at all accidental, and I began edging away.

After lunch we all went down to the beach. For some reason, I never knew beforehand that Ted, his sister, and her husband had blown up a yellow raft and headed into the ocean. By myself, I waded into the water and was soon thigh deep. With no particular plan, I intended to frolic a bit before returning to the sand.

Until that day I'd spent many hours seaside in San Clemente, California, once more dropped off by Mother to spend a month with the

Helen Healy family, whom she considered her close friends. Like the family's three red-headed kids, Allan and I spent whole days at the beach, where we bounced through Pacific Ocean waves, tumbled freely, then surfaced into clear air. Since we always rose to the top, none of us felt any fear.

But that afternoon at Jones Beach everything changed.

I was standing in water below my waist when a strange sensation struck me—the water exerting a kind of peculiar pull. I pivoted to escape, to make my exit to dry land, when suddenly I felt sand sliding beneath my toes … as though the ocean floor was skidding away. A terrifying sensation. *But why?* I wondered. *I'm just trying to get back to shore.*

Then, to my horror, I could no longer touch bottom. The water was now so deep I had no recourse but to swim. I rolled over to my stomach, in full panic mode, and tried to stroke back to the beach. But to no avail. Making no progress, I could see the land was backing away. The ocean had somehow trapped me.

With no idea what was occurring, overcome by unalleviated terror, I swam uselessly until I became fatigued. Which was when I saw the fat doctor bobbing nearby, also caught, apparently, by whatever was happening. I called out to him. "Can I hang on to you a minute—just to rest?"

"No!" he shouted. "No! Don't touch me!"

"Just for a minute," I begged. *I won't drown you.*

"No. Stay away. You stay away."

My last hope for respite gone, I turned over on my back, hoping I could merely float. As it turned out, I could. For awhile, now almost numb, I watched waves forming high over my head, imagined they would collapse over my face, then felt myself picked up and somehow raised out of the way. Strange how they lifted me instead of drowning me.

Some illogical part of my brain began to wonder how long it would be before I reached the opposite shore … while the rational areas knew this was both silly and impossible.

Curious, I turned again onto my stomach and experienced a huge new wave of fear. The beach was now so far away the people had become miniatures. How far out was I, anyway?

Unable to bear the sight, I reverted to my back and floated once more.

Suddenly another human entered my vision. "Are you all right?" a man called out, and I saw a lifeguard beside me, swimming easily, since he was equipped with a long yellow flotation device. A kind of rubber banana.

"I'm alive," I said, imagining he would now rescue me. He didn't. Instead, with no further words, he disappeared and I was once more alone.

About then a strange sound reached me from somewhere—a man shouting across the water, "HELP!" And then again, louder, more drawn out, "HEEELLLLP!"

Vaguely I wondered who it was. Clearly that person was far away, so distant that I'd never be able to spot him. For a moment I considered making the effort to yell for help myself, but gave that up as useless. Nobody would hear a little girl with a twelve-year-old voice.

Time stretched endlessly, and yet collapsed inward. Stark terror can last only so long. I was strangely calm, now sure I would die. I just didn't know exactly when. Above me the ocean rose in giant waves, lifted me up, then once again dropped me down in a hollow.

Once more I heard those strange cries for help.

Sometime in that Dying Soon mode, another vision appeared. This time it was a wooden boat full of men. Before I fully grasped what was happening, masculine arms reached down and pulled me up over the edge and dropped me down inside.

I had no idea this was a Coast Guard boat.

Still consumed by pent-up fear, I had no emotions left, no capacity to feel excitement or even relief. I sat there, wet and dull. At the moment it was just another thing that happened, once more out of my control.

Minutes later, they pulled in the fat doctor. Repelled, I pulled my legs out of his way.

Just as it dawned on me that I might live after all, one of the men in the front of the boat stood up. "Goddamit!" he shouted to the others, "when I say row to port, you row to port. Now ROW! TO PORT!"

He shot a quick glance behind him and I suddenly perceived the problem. The boat was sweeping toward a rock jetty, fast and seemingly out of control. The rocks were there waiting.

The head oarsmen howled again. "ROW! Dammit! ROW!"

The rock jetty came up fast. Then faster.

Oh God, I thought, *we're going to crash. We'll die after all.*

The six men strained and pulled and grunted. The jetty was upon us. And then it wasn't. At the very last second the boat swept around the ocean-most end, and back into clear water.

For a second the men laid down their oars and took deep breaths. Nobody cheered.

From then on, the boat seemed to do what it pleased. It whirled around, changed directions aimlessly, even stopped for a second, as though in a confused sea. Then, for reasons I never understood, our craft suddenly and inexplicably headed for land. Fast, and then faster. A crowd stood there, waiting. Hundreds of people, it seemed.

Our boat swept up on the sand and ground to a halt.

JUST WHEN I THOUGHT ALL THOSE PEOPLE WOULD LIKE TO MEET ME, the heroine who had lived through terrible danger and saved her own life, the fat doctor grabbed my arm. He propelled me out of the boat and past everyone up onto firm sand. All the while he shouted, "No publicity! No publicity!"

I tried to jerk away. After what the ocean did to me, I *wanted* some publicity.

Nobody moved fast enough to catch us. The fat doctor made sure of that. From then on, I hated him more than ever.

Farther up the beach we caught up with my family.

"I was so scared!" I cried out as we approached Ted, Margaret, and Art. "I was out in the ocean—way out," and my father replied, "So were we, Maralys. And we were scared too."

I stared at him. "You were out there—with me?"

"Yes. We were helpless. We were swept out and couldn't get back. We began shouting for help."

"That was YOU? Your voice I heard?"

He smiled, but he looked exhausted. "Mine and Art's. I thought we were the only ones."

"The Coast Guard came for me. And ... " jerking a thumb backwards, "him too. How did *you* get back?"

He shrugged. "The ocean changed its mind and swept us toward shore. All we had to do was hold on." He glanced at his sister. "We put her on the raft. Art and I held onto the sides. That's when the ocean suddenly reversed itself and rushed toward land, faster than we went out. By then we didn't need to be rescued."

None of us ever learned whether it was we two swimmers or the shouters gripping their raft who finally brought the Coast Guard.

But one thing we realized immediately. Still consumed by churned-up fear, all of us needed to spend hours talking, re-living the experience.

Ted said, "We should tell our story to a reporter, they'll want it in the newspapers," and his doctor friend made a face and said, "Never! We don't need publicity!"

Ted ignored him. Later a journalist appeared at Ted's cottage ... and nobody cared that Ted's friend saw him coming and suddenly left. I overheard my father and his brother-in-law saying, "Something's going on with that man."

Talking helped relieve our powerful emotions.

But fear like that was not easily dissipated. It had to be explained, recounted, re-experienced. For hours we re-played the drama, augmented by our tension. Ted said, "We were caught, you know, in a Sea Puss." He shuddered. "I never want to experience that again. Ever."

My aunt said, "You were a brave girl, Maralys. I'm proud of you. Such a response to an awful horror. I couldn't have done it myself. I would have tried, but you were pluckier than I ever could have been."

"Really?" I smiled at my aunt, with her magic ability to make me feel we were both the same age.

Later she pulled me aside. "Honey, let's go sneak some ice cream."
I'd always adored her. But right then I loved her more than ever.

FOR THE NEXT FIVE YEARS I HAD OCCASIONAL NIGHTMARES, WAKING in terror as I felt the sand once more sliding between my toes.

Much later I was to learn that nobody out West had ever heard the term Sea Puss. Everyone in California corrected me. They said, "That was just a riptide."

Ultimately, that's not all people said. "You could have gotten out of it," listeners claimed. "You never swim toward shore, you know. You escape from a riptide by swimming sideways."

As a mature adult, I've examined that idea in detail and now realize it's nonsense. When a powerful ocean force has you in its grip, pulling you out to sea, and then sweeping right and ultimately back to shore, tell me how it's possible to swim sideways out of this great rushing arc. Do you stroke to the left, facing the moving current head on and trying to out power it? Or do you swim right, in the current's own direction, gathering enough speed to out pace the moving body of water?

Such a feat would have required, at the very least, an Olympic swimmer. Which was hardly me. And certainly not the me who was twelve years old. At the time, all I knew about ocean tides was nothing.

Just a year ago as I taught novel writing to adult students, I learned something else about oceans. My boating expert, Bob, who once fell off his own sailboat, said, "I was lucky my wife kept her eyes on me. In the ocean, even in the relatively calm Caribbean, a single swimmer is extremely hard to spot. Somebody on the boat has to maintain eye contact. Or you can be lost forever."

How, then, was I fortunate enough to be spotted in the turbulent Atlantic? A lone swimmer (well, two of us), far out to sea?

Looking back, it might have been the overweight doctor who made us visible—wallowing large, white, and blubbery.

In any case, my student's experience suggested it was more than guts that saved my twelve-year-old life. It was also luck.

FOR ME, THAT AFTERNOON AT JONES BEACH REMAINS ONE OF THE singular events in my life … an hour when I easily could have died—and knew it.

Although my husband and six kids are all good swimmers … some are snorkelers and others are scuba divers … I've never again trusted the ocean. Not even near shore.

If I enter the sea at all, just to snorkel, I go with a blow-up raft. And even then I'm wary and tremulous.

I beat the ocean once. *Which is quite enough,* I think, *for one lifetime.*

AS IT TURNS OUT, I'VE SAVED MY OWN LIFE A FEW MORE TIMES. AND once, thanks to the persuasiveness of my oldest son, I even risked it. He promised I'd survive—but once I was soaring above the earth at 2000 feet (without an engine or parachute) I didn't believe him.

LATELY I'VE CONCLUDED MY QUEST TO HOLD TIGHT TO THIS WOBBLY flagpole called Life, is … well, vital. If you're going to capture six generations of one family, you have to be around to do it.

CHAPTER TWO

It All Began at a Jolly-Up

A WIDE-EYED STARE ACCOMPANIED MY ADMISSION TO A NEW acquaintance that I'd married at age nineteen. We were trading backgrounds as we stood in the Tustin Presbyterian social hall, with people milling around. "Nineteen?" she repeated, and I could see her reaction, somewhere between disbelief and dismay—which I'd come to expect. "Seriously?" she asked. "Nobody marries that young. Not any more."

No, I was thinking, *They don't.* And I reflected on my own grandkids. "Today's young people just 'hook up'," I said, "and live together and don't bother with rituals." *And they're apt to repeat the process several times—which is like getting a divorce without the nuisance of paperwork.*

"Early marriage worked for us," I added with a shrug. "Neither of us ever looked back." I pondered the issue further. "Who can say, long run, which system gets the best results." After a pause. "What do you think?"

She smiled and shook her head. "I was widowed, just got re-married. So I'm no expert."

Privately I was thinking, *Somehow I believe that we, and our various friends who also married young, were more likely to make it to that venerated fifty years. There's something to be said for a relationship with strings attached.*

Later, after we'd parted, my thoughts hung in the ether. *We weren't crazy,* I mused, *it just happened he was the best thing that came along, so I grabbed him.*

Actually, I was his best thing, too.

For us, in spite of some rocky times, it turned out an early marriage worked to our advantage.

A few months ago he said, "We're like two trees, Babe, whose trunks have grown together."

I felt a surge of warmth and patted his shoulder. I cherish this image, and think about it often … except when I'm mad at him.

Of course I get mad at him. But only after he gets mad first—which is the natural order between the guy with the short fuse and the gal with too many "feelings."

Still, Rob and I learned years ago that most things aren't worth fighting about. We both know where we stand on almost everything, and where we stand is mostly on the same tightrope.

During my second year of college, Rob and I met at a Stanford "Jolly-up," a Saturday night get-acquainted event … which for me, just starting summer quarter, was rife with possibilities.

As I fished in the dorm closet for a dress, my roommate turned to me with a look of scorn. "I wouldn't dream of going," she said. "It's nothing but a meat market." She sat at a small vanity, studying herself in the mirror. "You're nearly a Junior. Why would you subject yourself to that?"

"I want to meet a guy," I said, "someone new." I turned to her. "Aren't you tired of all the men who have nothing to say—except where they got drunk last weekend and where they plan to get drunk next weekend?"

She shrugged. "What do *you* want to talk about?" With a quizzical stare. "World affairs?"

"That would be okay with me."

She turned away. "Go find your egghead," she said. "I'm staying right here."

So I went. And indeed I did meet a thinker, but he wasn't an egghead, and never mind my first impression, that he was too short, and my second, that he brimmed over with personal questions, too many for a first encounter. In spite of all that, I found his willingness to talk, his bright expression irresistible.

Eventually I learned what *he'd* been thinking that night; at least this is what he told me later:

As I stood on the sidelines watching the dancers, my eye caught one girl in particular. Tall. Sexy and lively. But making a fool of herself, putting on a show. She needs rescuing, I thought. I'll cut in on her.

She hadn't seen me coming, gave me a surprised look. But she was easy to dance with, easy to talk to. We seemed to have a lot in common, both of us with gypsy backgrounds. After a few dances, I wondered aloud who was walking her home. Another look of surprise.

Isn't going to happen. I withdrew the question and regrouped … asked what she was doing the next day.

Before she could answer, I pushed ahead, asked if she'd like to go on a beach party. Obviously I'm throwing her. She hesitates, finally agrees. Wasn't sure she would.

Back in my dorm room, I re-live the dance, reflect on what I see in her, write a note and take it to her box. She might as well know what I'm thinking.

What I'm thinking next is, With no car, how do I work out this beach party?

THAT NIGHT I WALKED HOME WITH SOMEONE ELSE. BUT ROB'S WAS the only face I remembered.

Next morning I found a note in my box. I stood in the lobby, reading Rob's note and blushing. He began, "You remind me of a former love …" *Oh, Lord. Last night too many questions: now this—too many embarrassing thoughts.* I fled to my room, still blushing.

The day grew worse.

Just as I reminded myself that a "party" meant other people—and guys who might be taller and wouldn't write awkward notes—I came downstairs to a startling scene.

No beach partiers anywhere. But waiting near the curb with its door open was a black Model A, complete with a no-expression driver.

Oh, and Rob as well, standing there smiling.

I stared at the car. "Where's everyone else?"

"Not sure what you mean." He shrugged and pointed. "This is Hudson Bowlby," he said, and gestured me inside. (Only later did he admit, "This was the only car I could get my hands on.)

Reluctantly, I slid across the narrow black seat, leaving scant room for Rob, who had to squeeze in beside me. Three was definitely a crowd. *I can't believe this. I'm stuck here in this old … machine.*

Looking straight ahead, Bowlby started the car, and the ancient crate began coughing its way down Memorial Drive.

For awhile we didn't talk. Finally I asked, "Who are we meeting at the beach?"

Rob turned to me in surprise. "No one. Just us."

"Just us?"

"Sure. What did you expect?"

Not this.

He changed the subject and eventually we began talking about America's problems … while Hudson Bowlby stared at the road, about as talkative as an English butler.

Rob and I carried on without him. We found we agreed on War. Peace. Money. Racial Discrimination. And Students that Smoked.

Miles later, with an effort, I turned sideways and noticed he had a great profile. In fact, he was handsome. I felt free to ask, "You call this a beach party?"

"Sure, Babe." He grinned. "I've brought grape juice and bananas and cheesy crackers. And we're going to the beach."

ROB NEVER BECAME A "NORMAL" BOYFRIEND. HE NEVER SUMMONED me with the dorm buzzer. Instead, he stood under my window and whistled, as though calling his dog. He never brought flowers or candy. He never apologized.

But he talked. And he also listened.

Rob's biggest problem couldn't be solved: he was too short ... only six feet tall, while I, at 5'10", had vowed never to date anyone whose eyes were even with mine. At dances I stuck to a kind of high water mark, never glancing at men shorter than 6'2".

After awhile, when we spent hours in the Stanford library passing philosophical notes back and forth, ("I'm getting nothing done," he wrote, "Let's leave"), or on afternoons when we sat under a tree and talked, or on weekends when we rode our bikes to the movies, I stopped noticing that he'd never met my height requirements. A powerful mind made him seem taller.

By quarter's end, one of us flunked out. Rob's "C" in Qualitative Analysis and "D" in Organic Chemistry (each a year's worth of work condensed for the summer), came as only a partial shock when you consider he'd picked the wrong subjects for the wrong semester.

Courtship takes time ... and so does weighing tiny grams of chemicals on delicate little scales, not to mention memorizing complicated carbon chains for organic chemistry.

In the end, Stanford gave him a choice: "Go down to San Jose State," they said, "bring up your grades, and come back."

I hadn't known him long, hadn't yet experienced his powerful inner pride. Rob said, "I'll go down to San Jose, all right, but I'm not coming back." And thus, for the fall quarter, I was there by myself—having escaped expulsion only because I applied for an Incomplete in Creative Writing.

To tell the truth, during that courtship summer I could easily have flunked out too; for my demanding, five-unit English course, weeks went by when nothing came to me ... except anxiety as I noticed other students handing in pages.

Finally, in a fit of terror, I sat down one night and began an intense, slice-of-life scene about poor people in a bar. Soon my thoughts started to flow. By the end I assumed the piece was so poignant the professor would be lavish with praise and inspire me to further greatness.

My instructor saw it differently. "Not bad for its sort," he scribbled across the top, "but its sort has been overdone." Elsewhere he jotted, "Hackneyed," an adjective I understood all too well. I was crushed … from then on devoid of ideas and clearly on the path to my own "D," saved from expulsion only because of that Incomplete.

In the end, my problem with that one submission may have been that I'd never been in a bar … and I didn't know any poor people.

It was Rob's commute along Bayshore Highway—in his green, humpbacked turtle of a car—that ultimately changed our lives. One Saturday as we were sitting in Manning's Coffee Shop in San Francisco, Rob said, "I'm tired of this long haul from San Jose to Stanford. All those hours on the road, Babe, just to get together. It's wearing me out." He stopped for a moment, then said offhandedly, as though he'd never given the subject a moment's thought, "We might as well get married."

I could hardly believe what I'd heard. A proposal. Well, almost a proposal. But for me it was enough. Having never given the subject any thought either, I said with too much enthusiasm, "Why don't we, Rob?" Then, laughing, "We could, you know."

Leaning closer, we plotted out reasons why it might work. "My folks are paying for my education now, Rob. They'll probably go on doing it."

"And I've got the G.I. bill—which won't go away." He gave me a certain look. "I think we can swing it, Babe."

And thus, at the change of quarters we were married by a Judge in his home, and together we finished the school year at San Jose State.

We shouldn't have been surprised that for the next two quarters we both earned straight "A"s.

It was Rob who decided we should transfer to UCLA.

I looked at him in dismay. "Let's go back to Stanford," I said, but he wouldn't hear of it. "I'm through with that school."

"I loved Stanford. I've always wanted to get my degree there."

"Go back, then. I'm transferring to UCLA."

"Without me?" I could hear myself whining. "You'd really go without me?"

He changed the subject. "I've always wanted to live in Southern California. I like to bodysurf, and the ocean is warm down there." Then with a smile, "You'll love it, Babe. And besides, UCLA is a good school."

He was right about the school.

But our lives that semester proved so complicated we never went near the ocean. Our studies were too demanding. And besides, at the start of fall quarter I discovered I was pregnant.

Chapter Three

Misled by Grantly Dick-Read

Pregnancy, like everything else, was different in 1949. Today, women attend college in full pregnancy mode and think nothing of it.

Not so back then. Nobody knew what was wrong with me when I sat in psych class slowly swinging my leg back and forth, and hugging myself because I was so nauseated.

One day I could no longer sit there quietly, pretending to be well. I jumped up, ran out the door, and right outside found an empty field. Aware that lying on my stomach sometimes helped with nausea, I dropped down into the earth and weeds.

But I was too far gone. Unable to hold back, I reared up and vomited mightily into the foliage. It wasn't pretty, but at least I was out there alone.

Or so I thought.

When I rose again, now feeling better, I noticed something I hadn't seen earlier. Looming a number of yards behind me was a large building circled by an ample porch, and on the porch stood a whole classroom full of young students, all staring down at me in wonder.

Embarrassment flooded through me; *oh Lord, I've made myself a spectacle.* An older version of me might have nodded and smiled. Instead I escaped back into my building, blushing and mortified.

Happily, Rob offered a special comfort for those nausea days by taking me out for meals. For lunch we went to the UCLA cafeteria, where I powered down the only food that seemed appealing—tomato soup. "No problem, Babe," he said when I thanked him. "We'll come again. I kind of like the food here."

As THE SCHOOL YEAR PROGRESSED, OTHER MORTIFYING MOMENTS presented themselves—though none that offered more than a startled gasp and a tale to recite later to Rob.

It was my mom's mother, Grandma Alice, who sent the cotton maternity dresses that wrapped me up like a burrito tied with strings. For awhile I was grateful.

But then I expanded. And too often the dress didn't.

As I carried notebooks and books across the UCLA campus, I sometimes felt something tickling the backs of my legs. It always took a couple of seconds before I grasped the problem. *Oh Lord, not again!*

Invariably I looked down to find the inner and outer strings had come untied—or broken—and the wrap-around dress no longer wrapped. Instead it had popped apart, creating loose ends that flapped against my ankles. Which left me staring down at my protruding belly, clothed only in underwear.

Hurriedly I juggled books and gathered up the trailing sides of the garment and pulled them around me ... though often I simply had to hold my maternity dress together until I could find a safety pin.

Later, I was given skirts and tops, but the skirts had a way of riding up over my expanding girth, revealing more leg than seemed decent. Increasingly, male students opened doors as I approached, then shrank back, as though to avoid any suggestion that we were together.

By the end of the semester in late June, I'd become something of a spectacle on the UCLA campus. I suppose other women would have given up and stayed home.

Not me. I wanted to graduate.

And so I did, in a male's extra-large commencement gown, which only barely closed in front. Ralph Bunche was our graduation speaker, offering a message I can't recall—though I can still hear Rob and his male friends

30

bantering among themselves about how, any moment, one of them would have to don gloves and deliver a baby.

My due date was upon us, yet the baby must have been enjoying a free ride, because he hung around an extra three weeks, all past my doctor's estimate.

Even before birth, our first child began making the rules.

JUST AS PREGNANT WOMEN DIDN'T ATTEND COLLEGE BACK THEN, childbirth in those days was different ... no, let's be honest, it was worse.

Eager to have the world's most perfect baby, I read *Childbirth Without Fear*, by Dr. Grantly Dick-Read ... about how wonderful it was to deliver an infant with no anesthetic ... how good for the child. And how, in fact, with the right relaxation and cheerful mindset, the process could be accomplished with so little pain.

During the last month, I curled up with the book balanced on my personal shelf and read phrases like, "Primitive women are rarely troubled by anxiety states or *toxic manifestations.*" Whatever that meant. And further, "Healthy childbirth was never intended by the natural law to be painful."

I should have taken greater note of sentences like, "Native woman ... she receives the impatiently-waited indications that her child is about to arrive ... isolates herself in a thicket ... undisturbed, she patiently waits."

Somewhere within those pages I found enough logic to bring Read's theories to the attention of my obstetrician.

On a late term visit I announced to Dr. Prucher, "I want to have this baby without anesthesia." By then I'd finished those startling pages.

"Really?" he asked, giving me a strange look.

"Childbirth isn't supposed to be painful," I pointed out. "If you relax, if you enjoy the process, it doesn't hurt."

"I see," he said noncommittally. "May I ask where you got this information?"

"From Grantly Dick-Read," I said, "from his book," and I didn't mention that Read subtly mocked the doctors who disagreed with him. Instead I burbled on, trying to bring Dr. Prucher into the fold. Clearly he needed enlightenment. Somehow it never occurred to me that a book was not the equivalent of having actually given birth. Or tending to hundreds of other births.

"An interesting viewpoint," he finally said, and I could see by his expression he not only wasn't convinced, he was barely listening.

"If that's how you want it, then, Mrs. Wills. We'll do it your way."

"Oh, good." At least he was cooperating.

Right then I should have said something about husbands needing to be there. A point I forgot to mention.

The reality was, in hospitals back then no support teams existed. Husbands weren't allowed anywhere near delivery rooms, or even pre-delivery rooms. Neither was anyone else.

For me, in those hours of labor, I was joined by exactly no one.

Alone in the dark, with no "thickets" around in which to hide, it was just me and my contractions.

After about an hour I was ready to forget I'd ever heard of a doctor called Read. Unlike what I'd read in his book, relaxation didn't seem to be working. Hey, I'd come into this room perfectly calm, full of relaxation, and yes, even good cheer.

Instead, Natural Childbirth began to bear down. I was shocked. The pain never retreated, not even for a moment. For me there were no "in-betweens," as the damned book had promised. No pain-free intervals to reflect on "natural law." Instead the pain just kept increasing. I should have read a childbirth book written by a mother.

Only occasionally did a nurse enter for a few seconds, poke me where it hurt most, and then disappear again. After a few hours even Dr. Prucher appeared—with the same painful internal exam.

I was trying to be brave. Trying every way I could to accept the agony and not give in. *For the baby. For the baby.*

Oh, damn the baby. I wished I'd never heard of Grantly Dick-Read.

My endurance slid away, then failed. Finally, to whomever appeared in the room around eleven p.m., some five hours after I'd arrived, I said, "I can't take this any longer. Please. Please give me … something."

A nurse came in with a shot. After that I went unconscious. It turns out I over-react to medications.

When I finally awoke it was noon the next day. Rob was standing by my bed, along with Rob's father, Art. Both were smiling. As I opened my eyes wider, wondering what had transpired, Rob said exuberantly, "It's a boy, Babe. And he's eleven pounds, three ounces." He grinned. "The biggest baby in the hospital. Probably in the county. Can you beat that?"

"Really? I've had the baby?" A surprise. "He's eleven pounds?"

"No, Babe. Eleven pounds and three ounces."

I smiled. Typical Rob. "Where's Ruth?" I mumbled.

"Oh, Mother. She's down in the nursery. Can't pull herself away from the baby."

Rob's words about Ruth and our baby were prophetic. From then on, she could never pry herself away from our children. Any of them. For good or for bad.

Whether Bobby Wills would ever become the world's most perfect baby, right then neither of us could predict. But he certainly became Dr. Prucher's largest-ever delivery ... and a surprise even to him.

I never spent another moment reading anything by Grantly Dick-Read.

Chapter Four

"Chub" Develops a Battering Ram

Alone! For the first time as an adult I'd be in an empty house … well, nearly empty.

Fall had come, and Rob was going off to Westwood without me. I followed him through the house. "I guess you're okay with getting back to the grind."

Ready to start at UCLA's new law school, he said as he went out the door, "Sure, I'm happy to be going, Babe. Why wouldn't I be?" I noted his low-key words—Rob recoiling from the emotionalism of his mother. Earlier he'd shown a glimmer of excitement. "Lucky I chose UCLA. The school has lofty ambitions. I keep hearing, *We'll be the Harvard of the West.*" He gave me a look. "Guess I picked right."

For a few minutes, as Rob drove away that first day of the semester, something hit me and I was shocked. I stood near our front door watching the green turtle disappear down the driveway and then down the street, suddenly feeling abandoned and insecure. Abandoned as my mother had dumped me so often—not just me, but also my brother, Allan.

Right then my stomach felt hollow and sickish. I was supposed to be a grown-up, but for a moment I was simply the left-behind child. Again.

With an effort, I gathered myself together and turned slowly to head back inside—into our small tract house in the San Fernando Valley.

Oh, yes, a little person was in there waiting for me, asleep in his bassinet. But he was new to me, too. And this mother thing. I'd never done that before.

Was I going to be good at it?

How on earth would I know?

THE ALONENESS DIDN'T LAST LONG. BEFORE NOON, ROB'S MOTHER, Ruth, showed up to help tend our baby, now named Bobby.

Ruth, with her attractive, dark hair, appeared at my door that day with a loving smile. "Oh, Maralys, where is that dear, dear baby!" Looking radiant, she virtually catapulted into the house.

But this was just her mood for that hour. Across her face flitted the emotion-of-the-moment, a caldron of ever-changing feelings that bubbled up from deep within.

"Oh, I must see him, the sweet little dear!" she cried.

Right then, I loved her very much. "Bobby's asleep in his bassinet," I said.

Later, when he awoke and cried, Ruth looked upset, and soon verging on desperate. "Feed him, Maralys. Poor little thing, he's starving. Look at him. Dear little Bobby." She hovered nearby, looking as if she might weep, too. "Oh … he's so hungry."

I didn't think he was quite *that* hungry. I took him onto my lap, unaware that soon I would cringe at her constant outpouring of feelings … she, who was never devoid of heartfelt, yet overwhelming facial expressions.

In an unguarded moment the day before, Rob had said, "Mother's quite the Drama Queen."

Ruth couldn't feed Bobby, of course, because I was nursing. But she hung over me, urging me on.

Of the three of us, only Bobby seemed disinterested in the goings-on. For that first month, Nature must have decreed that he confine his nursing to small sips … to make up for having arrived overweight and overfed.

I thought back to the hospital, how he filled the hospital crib, looking a month older than all the other infants … which explains why the nurses thought him hilarious, and kept teasing me with giggles and little jabs: "Is your baby going to walk home?" "I'll bet he knows how to read."

I smiled, but inwardly thought they were poking fun at our child … that perhaps they assumed I'd eaten too much and created a monument to piggery. (Which shows how little I knew then about gestational science.)

Since even to me our son seemed a tad past "cute" and well into "chubby," I couldn't wait to get him out of there and away from those joking nurses.

HOME AGAIN, AS THE PUFFINESS RECEDED, BOBBY BECAME TRULY handsome. Still, we nicknamed him "Chub." But nursing and extra cuddling didn't appeal to him. He sucked briefly, almost grudgingly, but he preferred pulling away and looking around.

Bobby introduced me to a style of motherhood I would never see again.

EVEN IN BABIES, PERSONALITY TRAITS QUICKLY BECOME OBVIOUS. Like most infants, Bobby wanted food and attention in the middle of the night. For awhile, maybe six months, I was up rocking and nursing him at least twice a night. Which was when my pediatrician said, "He needs to sleep through now. He's old enough."

"How do I make that happen?"

"Don't pick him up. Just let him cry. Or maybe go in once and pat him on the back, then leave. He'll get the idea. Pretty soon he'll fall asleep, and that will be that."

With Bobby, "that" was never "that." Tentatively, I tried, but the pats on the back proved useless. Instead, he cried plaintively, which meant I had to sit and rock him, spend an hour at one a.m., and then again at four, trying to get the reluctant sleeper to nod off.

The evening came when I made up my mind. "Tonight," I said to Rob, "I won't sit and feed him. No matter what."

"You can give it a try," he said. His skepticism was obvious. "We'll see how it goes."

That night Bobby proved who he was. After a pat on the back, I returned to bed.

It didn't work. He ramped up the wailing.

Rob and I lay stiffly under the covers, trying not to hear. "Are you asleep?" I whispered.

"No. Of course not ... Are you?"

The sobbing went on. Loud, then louder. Bobby was not about to give up. For an hour he cried, he howled, and finally he screamed in rage. Rob and I were miserable. We could tell our baby was as determined to make me come as I was determined not to go.

That awful hour became two hours. And then suddenly, around two and a half hours, silence, then the sound of an ominous thud.

I jumped up and ran in.

In his rage, Bobby had propelled himself over the high sides of the crib and landed on the floor. I picked him up, saw he was okay, and rocked him gently in my arms, then laid him back in bed. After that he went to sleep.

In my mind I'd become less than a fabulous mother.

The next night he cried for most of an hour. The third night for half an hour. Four nights later he finally slept through.

But there were still late night hours when Bobby felt he needed diversion. Instead of crying when he awoke, he began rocking his crib. Eventually he discovered if he rocked hard enough he could propel his bed across the bedroom floor. When he reached the far wall and out of traveling space, he turned his crib into a battering ram, bouncing it hard and repeatedly against the far wall ... *Can you hear me now?*

Those crib voyages, while less traumatic than angry wailing, were anything but peaceful. Both the crib and the floor, not to mention the wall, were under siege. At last Rob said, "Goddammit, I've had enough," and he nailed the crib to the bedroom's wooden floor—and try as he might, Bobby was forced to stop his midnight travels.

Naptimes evolved into other battles. When Bobby refused to sleep during the day, which was most of the time, Ruth became my naptime rescuer. "I'll just drive him around," she said, and settled him in her car and meandered endlessly through the neighborhood until he finally drifted off. For this, I was eternally grateful.

When our little boy refused to eat, I found myself chasing him around the backyard with spoonfuls of peas.

At times I wondered, *Is it me or is it him?*

How can a baby not yet a year old, be outsmarting Ruth, Rob, and me?

Only now, as I review distant memories, am I seeing Bobby in his entirety ... exceedingly bright, endlessly inventive, but born with a fierce inner drive that surpassed even my own innate stubbornness.

Yet Bobby outdid me on every front; he was ME, but in triplicate.

At nearly two, still a clumsy little fumbler, he was slow at getting dressed ... meaning I often had to take over because I was running late. Young as he was, Bobby refused to cooperate. "Do it by self," he insisted. "Do it by self."

If I persisted, the minute my back was turned he undid what I'd accomplished, undressed himself to precisely where I'd begun, and slowly, awkwardly, finished the job.

Some eighteen months after Bobby's birth, we had another son, Christopher Allan. Right from the start, everything about him was different. Though he, too, was large—a hefty ten pounds—from there on his resemblance to Bobby ended.

With Chris I went from being a flailing, semi-competent mother to a fairly good one.

I'd love to say it was because I'd learned so much about mothering from my first child. But that was simply not the case. With some kids you don't learn, you just cope.

The big difference was Chris himself. An angel must have said to him, "Go down there and do your best. Your mother needs all the help she can get."

CHAPTER FIVE

A Different Kind of Kid

BOOKS HAVE A WAY OF TAKING OVER MY LIFE. WHILE CHRIS WAS ON the way, I found myself hooked by yet another lifestyle "expert" ... this time caught up in the wisdom of author Adelle Davis, a nutrition guru who was highly regarded—make that worshipped—by readers intent on living forever.

Full of enthusiasm, Davis wrote a number of such books, ahead of her time in promoting dietary solutions to health problems. It was Rob's mother, Ruth, herself a health food nut, who arrived one day with Davis' *Let's Have Healthy Children.*

"You must read this, dear. I know you want another sweet child like Bobby."

"Sweet?" I said, thinking about Bobby's crib, currently nailed to the floor.

"Healthy," she amended. "Just read it, Maralys. You'll be amazed."

So I began. And indeed I was impressed.

Among Davis' admonitions was that pregnant mothers needed many extra grams of protein ... the only way, she explained, to produce an exceptional baby. She offered Brewer's Yeast as the perfect solution.

Has anyone today tried Brewer's Yeast? If not, I'll enlighten you; it tastes terrible.

Still, constantly nudged from those pages, I soldiered on, gulping down (make that gagging down), daily glasses of the awful stuff.

Those moments became pure punishment. Yet I persisted for perhaps a couple of months. Then one day the Yeast itself rebelled and came flying back.

That did it.

From then on, I ignored that part of her book.

I SOON DISCOVERED NOT ALL PREGNANCIES ARE ALIKE. I'D BEEN carrying this second baby for about six months when I discovered something odd. Whenever a sudden, loud noise or bang occurred in my vicinity, the baby inside me jumped—a startle response I could hardly believe. Between the two of us, he reacted first ... as though someone had given him a hefty nudge. It wasn't my imagination; it happened too often.

"What do you think this means, Rob?"

"No idea. You didn't notice this with Bobby?"

"Never."

He shrugged. "He must have good hearing. Or a finely-tuned nervous system."

That wasn't Chris' only response to trauma. For a few days after he was born, he actually ran a fever. I was so worried, I cried ... consoled only slightly when the pediatrician came into my hospital room. "I wouldn't be too concerned," he said. "This might be your baby's passing objection to getting born. It's an ordeal for them, too."

Which must have been the case.

From then on, Chris was under the influence of his secret angel, as though making up for all the stress caused by Bobby.

ANYONE WHO CARES ENOUGH TO READ ADELLE DAVIS WOULD OF course nurse her babies. Which I did, exclusively ... until Chris decided on his own to try something else.

One day, just after he'd learned to sit up, perhaps at about four months, I took him to the grocery store, plopping him into the seat on the wheeled cart. The store sold ice cream cones, so I bought a scoop of vanilla and began pushing the grocery cart as I licked. Before I'd gone far, two tiny hands reached up and pulled on my arm. Curious, I let him do it, let him lower the hand holding the ice cream.

The minute the cone came within reach, Chris plunged his face into it, his tiny tongue out as he sucked in the cold sweet stuff. It didn't bother him that his face disappeared … that from eyebrows to chin he was covered in ice cream. He just kept slurping.

A woman standing nearby burst out laughing. "You must have known he loves ice cream."

"Actually, I didn't know. He's never tasted it before. Or for that matter, any adult food. He just grabbed my arm."

"And you let him," she said, still laughing. With that she handed me a napkin. "Looks like you'll need this."

"Thanks," I said. "So much for keeping him on a diet of mother's milk!"

For his first halloween, I took Chris next door for a quick trick-or-treat. He was then eleven months old, already an experienced walker. Smiling, the neighbor said, "Here, you cute thing," and handed him a candy wrapped in cellophane. For seconds, Chris looked at the candy with a puzzled expression. Then he handed it back and said, "O-pen."

We both laughed, and our neighbor removed the cellophane.

Besides reading to the boys, I often added little poems, hoping they'd be entranced by the rhythm. At eighteen months, to my surprise, Chris recited one of them back to me—clearly enough so I was able to memorize his exact pronunciation: "Dis raining. Dis boring. Ol mon. Noring. Bump his head. Foo bed. Couldn't go up—in a morning."

For this performance, Rob and I laughed and clapped.

Soon Chris learned the tune and words to "Davy Crockett." Our next door neighbors, Bea and Tom Harding, heard him and were entranced. With that, Rob leaned a ladder against our backyard wall, and each day Chris climbed the ladder and sang "Davy Crockett" over the wall … loud enough so Bea Harding came out and gave him a cookie.

One day Tom said, "We hope you guys never move."

It's a Duck. And It's Dead!

With two babies in diapers and Rob away at UCLA law school, the laundry consumed too much of my day. Someone had given us an old washing machine, which was nothing more than an elongated metal tub which rocked violently side to side like an earthquake on legs. Slamming the diapers from one far edge to the other, it did part of what today's washing machines do, except this was agitation on steroids. Rob said, "I feel like I'm watching a carnival ride."

Next time friends came for dinner, Rob herded them to the garage. "If you want entertainment, come see our washing machine." And indeed, the contraption rewarded us once more by beating up on our clothes.

But the crazy machine neither rinsed nor spun. All that was up to me.

And then, as though reading my mind, my mother's rich father, Russell, (my maternal grandfather), sent us a letter. Before I opened it, I sniffed the envelope. Years earlier, Mother had noted, "Dad keeps his stationery in a humidor, same place he stores his expensive cigars. Which is why his envelopes have an odor." Even traveling from the East Coast, a journey that must have involved trucks, planes, machines and human hands, those envelopes retained a rich, spicy aroma.

In his terse style Russell wrote, "Here, Maralys. Buy yourself a washing machine. And use the rest for soap." When I looked at the check, I gasped. In an era when washing machines cost less than $100, Russell had sent a check for $500. Which meant, back in 1952, the washing machine would consume only a tiny portion, leaving the rest for ... well, lots of soap.

Included in his wildly original handwriting, Russell issued a warning. After he congratulated the two of us on our second boy, he added a last thought: "I've never known a successful rabbit."

Rob and I read that line together and gave each other a look. He said, "In case you get pregnant again, Babe, we'll have to keep it a secret."

At the moment, we had no intention of becoming rabbits, successful or otherwise.

BEFORE I BEGAN THIS BOOK, MY GRANDDAUGHTER, CHRISTY (OUR son Chris' oldest daughter) contacted numerous East Coast relatives and said, "Tell me what you remember about Russell." And they told her.

She read family journals and newspaper articles. Ultimately she presented me with an outline of everything I wanted to know about my grandfather Russell and his Montclair, New Jersey, family as he was growing up.

To my surprise, the antics of Russell's four brothers and one sister bore an uncanny resemblance to the mischief and craziness Rob and I lived through as we raised our own five boys and a girl.

Whether it was by sea or by air, the passion for adventure that drove these two sets of young men was both startling, yet somehow strangely familiar.

Thanks to Christy, the next chapter skips to an earlier time ... a pause to re-live my grandfather's wild youth—but mostly to marvel at his four older brothers, all of whom spent their early years flirting with disaster.

CHAPTER SIX

Daredevils in Montclair

Montclair, New Jersey. 1881

THERE IS NOTHING MORE EXCITING, MORE RECKLESS, OR MORE unpredictable than a family with an oversupply of boys ... especially without the leavening effect of girls. The more boys in a family, the thicker the atmosphere of competition, thrills, bizarre experimentation, and edge-of-danger adventure ... all carried along on a rising tide of testosterone.

In 1881, my grandfather, Adrian Russell Allan, became the fifth boy in such an enclave—the family of a New York Dentist, George Smith Allan. Their only girl, Alice, trailed the five males by six years and ultimately left a record of her brothers' escapades—which strangely, yet predictably, resembled the antics of Russell's six great-grandchildren, five of them boys, several generations later.

After awhile, the hapless mother of such an unruly mob can retain her sanity only by frequent escapes. So it was no surprise that Eunice Ruth Allan, nee Davies, often fled to the home of her mother in a town called Fishkill.

But she could never escape completely.

AS THE MOST OBSERVANT SCRIBE IN THE ALLAN FAMILY, AND CLEARLY fascinated by the events swirling around her, young Alice faithfully recorded the shenanigans of her older brothers. "Once more," she wrote, "as happened so often, Mother was in Fishkill. Peace reigned on the domestic scene, with Percy (the second son) dutifully mowing the lawn. Fred (the third boy), wanted to play and tried all manner of inducements to get Percy to leave the grass and do something more entertaining—but no, Percy was going to finish the job ... So Fred lay down on the ground, stuck out his hand, and dared Percy to come on.

"And Percy came on. The mowing machine was sharp and it neatly sliced off Fred's first finger.

"Fred held up the finger, dangling (as he claimed), on a shred of skin and wagged it up and down. 'Now see what you've done!' he cried. Whereupon Percy called for Charley, the oldest boy, who ran to the stable and hitched up the horse, bundled Fred into the buggy and drove to the doctor's office as fast as the horse would go—while Fred held onto his finger.

"The doctor took one look and said, 'Why, Charley, I can't save that finger. There's nothing to do but take it off.'

"'You've got to save it,' said Charley firmly, "Mother is in Fishkill.'"

"To keep him quiet, the doctor stitched the finger as best he could, with no idea that it would stick.

"Clearly," Alice finished, "the finger was not as near severed as Fred claimed, because it grew on again nicely, and though it was always a bit stiff, Fred could use it perfectly."

During the dentist's early years with a houseful of boys, the family planned a summer vacation in Narragansett. Alice writes that the mother and her (then) five boys traveled on a boat with "two or three maids and trunks and bags to match." But the dentist chose instead to take a leisurely train from New York, because, as he said, "I don't want to travel with a circus."

It is ironic that nearly 100 years later, that term surfaced again when our household was described by my husband as "A Circus without Elephants."

IT IS DURING THE WILD YEARS IN HER FAMILY THAT ALICE RECORDS another caper. As brothers bent on mischief will do, if they can't involve someone within the family, they conveniently find a boy on the outside. Alice writes: "About this time Percy used to play with an evil boy named

Jasper Rand. Jasper, the son of the Rand Drill Company's owner, was a great pet of one of his father's foremen, who kindly gave him sticks of dynamite.

"He and Percy had a wonderful time experimenting. One day they dug a hole under the roots of a big tree, put in a piece of dynamite, lit the fuse and ran. Up went the tree, as straight as a moon rocket, and came down neatly to the place it had started.

"Encouraged by this success, they looked around for something bigger, and found just the thing in a great rock in Jasper's backyard. They dug down the side of it, and dug and dug, but the rock went down indefinitely. Finally, worn out from their efforts, they held a consultation and decided to put the dynamite at the bottom of the hole and not try any longer to get under the rock.

"They put down a stick, lit the fuse once more, and dashed away. They thought that dynamite blows up vertically, but not so—it explodes equally in all directions. So, as it hit the rock at an angle, the rock rose up in a graceful curve, sailed lightly over the fence and came down on the next yard—right onto the neighbor's outhouse. The father, just emerging, looked back in horror, knowing he'd escaped with his life.

"When the results of this experiment came to Mother's ears, she announced that Percy did not need any more lessons in physics, and Percy found his friendship with Jasper brought to an abrupt end."

Her mother's ability to end such a friendship suggests that mothers of her day had considerably more power over their children's attachments than they did a hundred years later.

It was the next-to-last son, Eddie, whose life was seriously threatened by a sailing expedition on Lake Ontario. As a student at Cornell, he'd paddled his canoe on Cayuga lake … but then, according to Alice, "was inspired to go on to greater things. He and two other boys figured out a scheme of sailing up the lake to the north end and then through the Erie Canal to Buffalo, camping on the shore at night, and then crossing Lake Ontario to Kingston.

"Eddie dutifully wrote home for permission: Mother said 'NO' loudly and firmly and made sarcastic remarks about the Owl and the Pussy Cat and 'characters who sailed away for a year and a day on a beautiful pea green boat,' but Father said, 'Oh, let him go. Eddie is a good sailor.'

"So, with the high command divided, Eddie and his friends went on with their plans. They rented a sail boat and sailed merrily to the North end of Cayuga and then went through the short connecting canal to the Erie Canal. They suddenly discovered something that had never occurred to them in all their poring over maps—the Canal was too narrow to tack!

"So they took turns trudging along the tow path, pulling the boat with a rope … a long, long way to Buffalo.

"They finally arrived there, dragged the boat through the Welland Canal and at last embarked on Lake Ontario. They set their course for Kingston and were soon appalled to find themselves out of sight of land. 'No one ever told me,' Eddie said plaintively, 'that Lake Ontario was so big.'

"Night came on, it grew darker and darker and a thunderstorm broke, apparently right over their heads. Never had they seen such bright lightning, such black darkness between flashes, or heard such loud, resounding thunder.

"Nothing to do but plow up and down the waves, keep headed for Kingston as well as they could and hope that somehow, some time they would come to land.

"After what seemed hours, the thunder grew fainter and farther off and the stars shone down on them. And at last they hit Kingston—right on the nose."

THOUGH ALICE OUTLIVED HER YOUNGEST BROTHER BY MANY YEARS (and presumably the other boys, too), she seemed not to notice that the greatest risk-taker of all—and the only sibling whose affairs would later be routinely tracked in the New York Times—was the fifth son, her nearest brother, Russell.

While Russell lived a less dangerous, less physical life than his older brothers, as an adult he became notorious for behavior that verged on reckless.

CHAPTER SEVEN

The Inscrutable Patriarch

Montclair, New Jersey Early 1900

MY GRANDFATHER, ADRIAN RUSSELL ALLAN, WAS DESTINED TO BE a one-of-a-kind rich man. Raised with those four older brothers who made no pretense of being Good Little Boys but routinely courted danger (the mowed-off finger, the near-disaster on Lake Erie, the dynamite), it seemed foreordained that my grandfather would also be something of a risk-taker.

After some years at Columbia, class of 1901, (no record exists that he graduated), Grandfather Russell decided to make his fortune on Wall Street.

In those days, when the New York Stock Exchange was still, literally, outside on the curb, Adrian Russell Allan considered his prospects and borrowed five hundred dollars. Eventually, through time and careful investing in such stocks as General Electric, Merck, and Dupont, he parlayed that sum into millions. But his behavior suggests he wasn't satisfied with a mere few million. Instead, reverting to the chance-taking mode of his childhood, he bought and sold with a gambler's instincts, so that over the years his fortunes ebbed and flowed. Family lore suggests that at times Russell Allan was worth at least $50 million.

In November 1904, Russell married Alice Lockhart Wilson, thus (with a sister of the same name), surrounding himself by ladies named Alice. On September 5, 1905, his first child, my mother Virginia, was born. Eventually they also had a second daughter, Katherine, and then a son, Sam.

Raised as a pampered child, "constantly attended to in his early years by maids and nurses," according to his sister, Alice, Russell gathered enough wealth to perpetuate his cocoon of comfort. Few of us, in fact, ever saw him in a solo setting; instead, he was the central figure for knots of hovering waiters, cab drivers, and bell boys, all awaiting handouts.

Stories about my grandfather Russell abound. In his early years, hiding behind deep blue eyes and a quizzical, noncommittal expression, Russell excelled at creating drama while pretending he wasn't involved. My mother recalls a beachside vacation at Quoque, which her father arranged for himself and a group of her college friends, both male and female.

"That first day," she said, "my dad set up camp in the lobby, and began handing out room keys. We could see a sly grin on his face, but none of us knew what the Cheshire Cat was up to. When we arrived upstairs, the reason for his smirk became clear. In our various suites he'd deliberately installed boys in the same quarters as girls, and now he refused to make changes. For his own amusement he'd created a scene right out of *It Happened One Night*.

In that era of sexual prudery, the women didn't think it funny, nor did most of the men.

"We women—and even the guys—found ourselves hanging towels from the ceiling, re-arranging and draping chairs, trying in every way to create modest barriers between the sexes so we could all undress in privacy.

"I ran downstairs to confront him. 'Why did you do this, Dad? You've embarrassed all of us.'

"'Really?' he said, 'Well, isn't that amazing!' And that was all he said. But his head was tucked into a newspaper and from the side of his face I caught the remnants of a grin."

THOUGH AT ANY GIVEN MOMENT RUSSELL COULD BE EXCESSIVELY rich or merely well off, his children were never aware of the distinction and probably didn't know that his name appeared sporadically in the financial section of the day's newspapers.

With each fresh accumulation of a fortune, Russell Allan bought a new yacht, boats on which he scarcely spent any time, and which he quickly gave away. It is said that over the years he donated yachts to several United States presidents.

In 1929, by selling off his stocks at a critical moment, Russell Allan not only contributed in his small way to the stock market crash, but rode through it unscathed. The deeper, sadder meaning is that he and his family were rich when most families in the United States were abysmally poor.

As the country plunged into desperate times, his daughter, my mother Virginia, sampled a tiny part of the depression. She happened to be driving her open-roofed Cabriolet through the streets of New York City when suddenly a man leaped into the car beside her. Before she could push him away, he raised a gun to her chest and demanded, "Give me all your money."

Startled, Mother stared at him, noticed that his voice quavered and his gun hand shook. She stuck out her own hand. "Give me that gun!" she demanded, as though speaking to a child.

To her surprise, the man handed it over. "You're not a killer, I can see that," she said.

To her further surprise, her assailant began to cry. "My family is starving," he said, trying to control his voice. "I would never have done this, but my children have nothing to eat."

Mother couldn't stand it. Reaching into her purse, she pulled out a fistful of bills. "Here," she said. "This is for your children. Now get out of my car." Then she added, "And take this horrible thing with you." Even as he was turning to leave, she made him take the gun.

For a second he seemed reluctant to touch it. But she was glaring at him, so he took it gingerly and jumped to the pavement.

Before she drove off, she saw him push the lid on a city trash can and thrust his arm down inside. She could only surmise that he had thrown away the weapon.

IN HIS MID-FORTIES, TO HIS CHILDREN'S DISMAY, RUSSELL DIVORCED his wife, Alice, and re-married, this time to a woman named Helen. As he matured, he became balder, ever more reclusive, and even more mysterious.

Within the family the Russell stories became legends. Mother describes the time her father met her train at Grand Central Station, and how, as she edged down the Pullman steps he took one horrified look at her suitcase and said, "Ginny, I won't have you carrying that disreputable thing." Reaching into his pocket, he withdrew a hundred dollar bill. "Here, Kiddy. Go get yourself a new suitcase."

Mother did (for much less than $100 dollars), but since the old luggage wasn't exactly useless, she gave it to a female cousin. Months later, Russell spotted the same suitcase with the cousin and once again handed over a bill, demanding that she buy herself a new one.

Rumor has it that the infamous suitcase earned four successive owners new pieces of luggage.

For me, as I grew up, my grandfather Russell had always been a mysterious character. Yet only as a pre-teen did I meet him in a setting I could recall. The scene took place in an expensive New York restaurant (they were always expensive), with Russell surveying the group from the head of the table, and other family members scattered along the sides. As always, he perpetuated his own air of mystery, regarding us with keen looks of appraisal and long silences. Few of us could even guess what he was thinking.

I realized at once that my very bald grandfather was the unspoken king, that in spite of his saying almost nothing, the whole restaurant was aware of his presence; a cluster of waiters hovered nearby, ready to jump at the raising of an eyebrow.

From time to time they crept closer and murmured, *What can we get you, Sir? Would you like another salad? Here, let me replenish your cocktail.*

Before we started, my grandfather picked up the menu. Eyeing each of us in turn, he held up the bill of fare and said, "Order whatever you want. Steak. Lobster. Anything."

So, for the first time, I tasted scallops.

"I love them," I cried, whereupon he decreed that I was to have more
… and almost before I'd finished the first batch, a second helping arrived.

With their appearance, I was suddenly bewildered. I'd already consumed as many of the little fellows as I could hold. Yet here came more.
Trying to remain inconspicuous, I simply stared at my plate.

Still, the scallop issue paled in comparison to Russell himself … a
shiny-headed man with that sharp, impenetrable gaze. His eyes were blue,
we could see that. Yet if he made one comment during the meal, I don't
recall it. Even back then I thought of him as a powerful, all-seeing sphinx.

My next memory of Russell took place when I was twelve,
then living in Berkeley, and anxious to receive a typewriter for Christmas.
Knowing I wanted to be a writer, Mother must have conveyed my wish to
both my father and grandfather, for at Christmas I was the recipient of two
brand-new portable typewriters.

My father sent a fairly inexpensive Underwood that was appropri-
ate for a twelve-year-old. But my grandfather secured the most expensive
Smith Corona then available. They made a vivid comparison as the two
sat side-by-side.

As always, Russell's gift came with an aura of prestige and power, as
though his present was routed straight from a Smith Corona showroom
on Fifth Avenue.

For some of us, having Russell in the family was like living
with a friendly Vesuvius. We never knew when he was going to erupt and
sprinkle us with lavish and unexpected gifts.

In time, Rob was treated to a grandfather meeting in person, and of
course Russell put the two of us up at the Waldorf Astoria, the only hotel
he considered worthy of a New York appearance. Of that visit, I recall
only one incident—the mortifying circumstances of our arrival. After the
bellman carried our bags upstairs to our room, Rob handed him a couple
of bills.

It is probably no coincidence that at that moment Russell appeared. As he watched the bellboy head away from our room, my grandfather asked, "How much did you tip him?"

"Two dollars," said Rob, which elicited from Russell a look of horror. "Two dollars!" he cried, and with alacrity I couldn't have predicted for a man his age, he wheeled abruptly and ran down the hall. "Boy!" he shouted. "Boy!"

Embarrassed for both of us, I stood in the doorway watching him go. Near the elevators, he caught up with his target. By then he must have been red-faced and panting. I saw him reach into his pocket and pull out a wallet ... saw a nod from the bellboy, saw Russell continue on to the elevators.

We never learned what my grandfather added to Rob's tip, but judging from past experience, this had to be a singular moment in the life of the bellboy.

Eventually I would glean that Russell paved his way through life with a lava flow of tips ... which accounts for the deference offered by those who served him.

Rob and I were too young, then, to give any thought on how long the Russell dynasty might last. For us, at the time, it seemed he'd be there forever.

Chapter Eight

Random House and Beyond

When I was first married, I seldom looked deep inside, almost never saw myself for what I was—a persistent, drilling down kind of German. Somehow I accepted my basic tendencies without noticing that when I got my teeth into something, I invariably held on.

But I didn't always pick the right fights.

At the top of my dream list, those early days in the San Fernando Valley, was a backyard covered in lush green dichondra. I'd seen it here and there—beautiful lawns with that curly, bright green groundcover that nobody had to mow.

My boys would love such a lawn, I thought.

For its size, our little house had a generous area in back, an invitation to the wonders of dichondra. But several negative features loomed from the start: a hard, clay-like soil that didn't encourage my pet grass's shallow roots. And worse, an infestation of that horrid weed called devilgrass.

Still, being the fighter I was, I set out to defeat nature and get the lawn I wanted. I soon discovered that devilgrass (technically, called Bermuda Grass) had tenacious roots that spread in every direction, so that whatever innocent green stems appeared on the surface were utterly deceptive. Underneath, the latticework spread wide and deep, like cancer, assuring that the above-soil product would last forever. And in the meantime, kill off anything as pure and innocent as dichondra.

Nevertheless, shovel in hand, I dug and dug, following the malicious roots wherever they led. Which, often enough, seemed bent on reaching China.

When at last it seemed I'd defeated a few square feet of lawn area, I planted large flats of dichondra. And then, of course, the second enemy emerged. Clay soil does not pretend to play gracious host to this lovely ground cover. Daily watering produced more mud than lawn. For well over a year I fought my losing, back lawn disaster. Which proved, in the end, to offer only one solution: move to a different house.

Along with cement-like, devilgrass-infested soil, came another problem with the San Fernando Valley. Heat.

Besides the fact that I don't perspire, meaning I'm miserable in hot weather, was the issue that nobody we knew had air conditioning. Instead, we homeowners filled half our windows with fans, some wet—called swamp coolers—some dry, and in mid summer we scooted around inside our houses with shades drawn, lingering mainly in the cool areas, meaning the few feet in front of one or another fan. In all innocence, I assumed all of California suffered the same punishing summers. Only later would I learn that *The Valley* was famous for its record-setting temperatures.

Once we moved to a different part of Southern California, I vowed we'd never again live anywhere near a region known to torture its residents.

Those early married years were also marked by Rob's decision to write a book. In the summer between his second and third years of law school—his last relatively free months before the start of a career—Rob began churning out hand-written essay pages. It fell to me to type them.

From the beginning, I was impressed. As I circled ever deeper into his manuscript, *The Need for a Rational Morality*, I perceived, once again, all the reasons I'd married him. Rob was a genius. "You're so logical," I said, "and what you say is so well written. I just know you'll impress an editor."

In his first paragraph, Rob outlined his intent: "This book is a pedagogical essay in the realm of moral philosophy, but written for public consumption. It is an attempt to pin down some of the trends in the field of morality or ethics which are disturbing to the author and millions of other Americans, and to tell why they are wrong.

"It becomes a rational argument against moral relativity and scientific, as well as dialectical materialism, and it proposes a rational, scientific approach to problems of ethics … to replace the declining ecclesiastical basis of Anglo-American morality."

Rob's thesis was that all the normal guideposts for morality seemed to be fading, starting with organized religion and including the traditional middle-class family. He argued that there had to be a new, rational basis developed for morality, starting with science, increased education, and codified life experiences.

In other places he mentioned psychological insight, and the need for individuals to be increasingly concerned about the need for ethics.

Deep within the first chapter he revealed his age—twenty-five.

Dazzled, I imagined Rob would soon be tapped by a major publisher. It seemed obvious to me that some decision-maker would immediately snatch him up and make him famous.

In between caring for Bobby and Chris (and inserted among those continuing battles in the backyard), I spent every free minute typing. At night, when it was time to quit, I'd go to bed with my brain afire and my limbs quivering with excitement. Rob's book was *so good*!

I couldn't wait to see him deliver his magical tome to a publisher. I could almost hear the editor showering him with praise, echoing the sentiments played out in my head.

Over the summer, the book and its pages grew—until finally Rob considered his treatise on morality as complete as it needed to be.

"Shall we mail it to Random House now?" I asked Rob.

"Oh, no," he said, horrified. "We have to deliver it in person, Babe. We certainly wouldn't want it lost in the mail." And, in fact, his fears did reflect the times. Photocopying had not yet been invented, so the loss of a carefully-typed manuscript would constitute a calamity.

So certain were we both of the book's acceptance, that we arranged a trip East, ostensibly to visit relatives—but mainly to stop at Random House and deliver his manuscript in person. It never occurred to either of us that we ought to call or write an editor first.

Brief as they were, our moments in Random House stand out vividly. As Rob and I entered the front lobby, with Rob carrying the manuscript box like a cherished treasure, he said, "May we speak to an editor, please?"

"Which editor?" the receptionist asked.

"Whoever handles serious topics," said Rob. He glanced at me, saw I was devoid of ideas.

"All our topics are serious," she said.

"A treatise on morality," Rob said. "Who would that be?"

She looked doubtful. "You can try Mr. Kline. He happens to be in right now." She pushed a buzzer. "He's busy, but he'll give you a few minutes."

She pointed us down the hall.

As we entered his office, Mr. Kline's head was bent over his desk.

Rob said, "Mr. Kline, I've written a book on ethics: *The need for a rational morality.*" With that, we half expected Kline to look up and express interest. Then, perhaps, to ask for the manuscript ... or maybe offer to discuss it. (In my wildest daydreams, I imagined an editor grabbing it out of Rob's hands).

Kline didn't do either. In fact the man barely managed to give us a glance. "You can leave the manuscript on my desk," he said, making no move whatever to encourage further conversation.

When we paused, he pointed. "Over there. Next to the ash tray. I'll get back to you."

Obviously we'd been dismissed. "Thanks," Rob muttered as he set down his precious ream box. Then, turning away, "Our phone number's inside."

Nothing further from Kline. We weren't sure he even heard.

The two of us departed the hallowed building in a vastly different mood. To say we were deflated would be an understatement. I, for one, was crushed.

Unlike us, our target hadn't been even slightly excited. And worse, he'd been unimpressed that we'd arrived in person.

Rob even said, "I think we might just as well have mailed it."

"But now I have only your notes," I said.

"True. But how often do boxes like that actually get lost in the mail?"

"It doesn't matter, does it? He'll call us soon," I said. "It's so good, Rob, I'm sure he'll want it."

BEYOND GETTING ROB'S BOOK BACK, FREE OF COMMENTS, WE NEVER heard from Random House again. I can only assume they must have mailed it, because we still have the original copy. But this is purely an assumption: one thing I do know—I never typed it twice.

For whatever reason, Rob never tried another publisher. Looking back now as an oft-published author, I can see we'd been as naïve about the industry as it was possible to be. The two of us broke every rule … including failure to get professional input on the manuscript, failure to make the title less stuffy and, most important, failure to try again.

But what did we know, the pair of us, just old enough then to think we knew everything?

A few years later I came much closer to publication with a humorous memoir. But I, too, gave up after only a few rejections. Had I grasped from the tone of editors' comments how close I'd been, that with additional re-working the manuscript might have yet found a home, it's possible I'd have been published years and years sooner than I finally was.

INCREASINGLY OVER THOSE EARLY YEARS, ROB AND I WERE THE recipients of my grandfather's beneficence. Even from a continent away we could feel his power, his generosity—and a sense that he loved wielding a magic wand.

Yet the two of us remained acutely aware of his one cautionary note: "I've never seen a successful rabbit." Thus we never told our benefactor when, nearly a year later, we learned we were having a third child. We knew we couldn't hide my pregnancy forever, but there was no need to prematurely ruffle his feathers.

On the day that I was in the hospital giving birth, Rob received a telegram telling us that Adrian Russell Allan was on the golf course—and that he'd just succumbed to a heart attack.

Both of us were shocked, and with that we renamed our new baby. Instead of calling him what we'd planned, Marcus Arthur Wills, we dubbed him "Eric Russell Wills." He was born September 5, 1953, which was also my mother's birthday.

Some years later Rob asked, "Babe, have you ever wondered how Russell would have reacted to our having six kids?" and I answered, "Does the word 'disinherited' come to mind?"

CHAPTER NINE

Moot Court Daze

OUR LOCAL NEWSPAPER SAID IT ALL: "UCLA STUDENTS, FATHER and Son, Graduate Together."

Rob's father, Art, newly retired from the Navy, had gone back to school to get a degree in history. "I'm here," he said, "so I might as well savor the full experience." Thus, for several years, Rob and I attended UCLA's football games at the Coliseum, crowing to ourselves that his father was down on the field with the drummers, the oldest student in the UCLA band.

That same year, 1953, Rob finished his three years studying law … as part of the second-ever class to graduate from UCLA's new law school.

In our family pictures I am standing next to Rob, but leaning against the law school's outer wall, smiling … and wearing an outfit that doesn't do much to conceal a serious pregnancy.

Rob and Art graduated in June, and our third son, Eric, was born September Fifth. Then, on October First, during a heat wave (in a downtown conference room with no air conditioning), Rob took the California Bar exam. Thus began an unsought family tradition of numerous momentous events piling up, one on top of another.

TWO BEDROOMS, AND NOW THREE LITTLE BOYS. I WAS NURSING, OF course, with Eric sleeping beside our bed in a bassinet. I asked Rob, "Once this baby leaves his little spot in our bedroom, where do we put him?"

Rob shrugged. "I don't know." Then he added, "Let's take another look at the garage."

The two of us stood on the cement in our one-car garage, grateful that our tiny tract house in Encino even *had* a garage. "Maybe we should create a room out here," Rob said. "Parcel off a section for Bobby."

Which we did, in effect stretching our house like a rubber band. Rubber-banding was what couples did when the father—even a lawyer-father—earned the magnificent sum of $350 a month.

Still, compared to other newly-graduated law students, we bordered on well-off. Rob now worked in downtown Los Angeles—in Liberty Mutual's Legal Department—at a salary enhanced by an event that eclipsed even the bar exam.

"Game Changing" is the only possible description for what occurred at the 1953 California Bar Convention.

Still exhausted after his three-day ordeal taking the Bar exam, Rob found himself once more competing as a finalist in UCLA's moot court competition.

The moot court event consisted of a carefully-crafted legal case submitted to most California law schools, in which selected students were assigned in pairs to represent the school and argue their side of the case in front of real judges … competing with students from another law school, who represented the other side of the case. After several such events a winning pair emerged.

But now several factors had changed: A) With the Northern California college winners having prevailed on the same side of the case as those from the South, the UCLA team lost the toss and had to switch sides. B) This was no longer a team event, but a competition among four finalists. C) The oral arguments would be held in front of all the lawyers attending the California Bar Convention in Monterey.

As we prepared to leave, with month-old Eric asleep in the backseat, Rob's mother stood at the curb, holding Chris on her hip and gazing down at us with a look of dismay. "You're so tired, Rob, why are you doing this? Oh, my stars, you shouldn't be driving all the way to Monterey! Rob, dear, tell them this is bad for your health! Just tell them! Please don't go."

Since she'd once begged Rob to quit law school … "It's so terrible, Rob, the way they make you work so hard. I'd just show them—and quit!" he placated her with a nod and a perfunctory response.

"I agree, Mother. It's terrible for my health. I'm not sure why I'm going to Monterrey either."

"Then stay home," she wailed.

"But I guess I gotta do it," he said, "since we've already signed up."

Ruth's expression never wavered. Still near tears, she waved half-heartedly as we drove away.

"Mother's always on the verge of collapse," Rob said. "At the moment she's worse than I am."

"But still, she's baby-sitting. Without her, we couldn't go."

"Yeah," he said. "I don't give her enough credit." He pointed to a file. "You'll have to take over the driving, Babe. I've got to study."

And then, after we'd shifted seats, "I'll be curious to see if there *is* another side to this case."

We'd started late, and soon it grew dark. "Can't see," said Rob, "and I'm not through with my analysis. How do I get this damn dome light to stay on?"

I tried to be helpful. "There's no dome light, remember? But the little light under the glove compartment goes on when you open the car door."

"I've just figured that out. But the door prefers to stay closed." Casting about, he muttered "Ah hah!" and leaning sideways, he cracked his door and kept it open with an Arden milk bottle. By a very dim light, he kept reading. And finally, "Maybe there *is* another side to this case," he said.

Once at the hotel lobby in Monterey, we ran into his erstwhile partner, Daren. "Hey, Rob, aren't you getting here kind of late?" he said. "We went to the cafeteria hours ago." He broke into a wide grin. "Just so you'll know—I've rented a trailer to bring home the winnings—all those law books."

Too tired to consider him funny, Rob just nodded.

That night baby Eric, unaccustomed to his new surroundings, kept waking up, howling. And I kept getting up to nurse him. Around five a.m., he finally fell into a deep slumber … precisely when a jack hammer started in the street below our window.

The alarm went off at seven, and Rob dragged out of bed, his expression dark, near homicidal. I raced downstairs to order breakfast. Ten minutes later, Rob arrived in suit and tie, took one look at the fried eggs and bacon and turned away. "Ugh. I can't eat that stuff. I'm sick."

Thus lacking both food and sleep, plus the better side of the case, Rob departed for the auditorium.

Twenty minutes later, after Eric was situated, I found Rob and three other men seated on the stage. I was thinking, *Oh, God, Rob, you look terrible. Exhausted. Please, just don't fall down. Don't disgrace yourself.*

Later, as the third contestant to argue, Rob rose and stood at the podium, gripping the edges and speaking in what I perceived as a calm but fainting voice. *Get through it, Rob. Please, just finish standing up.*

Worried beyond reason, I never heard a word he said.

Soon his part ended. Rob sat down again—still conscious. I took a huge, relieved breath.

One more speaker. Then, for awhile, the audience chatted quietly. Finally a judge came out front and said in solemn tones, "We've had four excellent arguments. A fine job by each of you." He paused, consulted a sheet. "And now the winner for the best oral argument is Robert Wills."

Astonished, I stared at the stage, tried to make sense of what I'd heard. Then, amidst the nods and clapping I muttered, "I don't believe it! I don't believe it!"

The lady next to me smiled.

But I couldn't contain my wonder, couldn't stop saying those same words over and over.

She patted my shoulder.

So Rob had won. But I could never figure out how or why it happened.

AFTERWARDS, LUNCH WAS ON THE BAR ASSOCIATION. WITH THE baby in my arms and Rob standing next to me, we smiled and smiled, said "Thank you! Thank you!" over and over. I'm not sure we ever ate.

WEEKS LATER, BOTH ROB AND DAREN WERE HIRED BY LIBERTY Mutual ... but thanks to his moot court win, Rob received an extra $50 a month.

FOR A SHORT TIME WE HAD THREE CHILDREN IN DIAPERS. THEN suddenly the number fell to one. Once Bobby began standing near the potty, Chris paid attention and simply imitated what he'd seen. To my delight, I was never involved.

With so many youngsters crammed into our tiny house, Ruth now became an almost daily member of the group. Yet even with her help we were constantly short of money.

Soon Rob's father also made frequent appearances.

One day Art said, "The papers are always talking about the Valley's shortage of teachers, Maralys. You've got a degree. Maybe you could be a substitute teacher. Mother doesn't mind babysitting."

"I'm all for it," said Rob. "It'll get you out of the house."

And so I entered the San Fernando Valley school system, quickly discovering that for me, substituting was ideal. A day here, two days there. Before the school kids had my number, meaning *Tall* doesn't necessarily equate with *Strict*, or even *Good on Discipline*, I'd be gone.

To my surprise, a few principals began requesting me.

Eventually, Rob said, "Why don't you get a teaching credential, Babe? So you'll know each day where you're going?"

THUS I WENT BACK TO UCLA FOR AN ADVANCED DEGREE. IN THOSE days it was Professor Corinne Seeds who held the hammer over all our heads. Among the requirements for a teaching credential was the dreaded "Seed Box," whose reputation terrified applicants long before I got there.

"Wait 'til you learn what that box is all about," a fellow student warned me. "It's a killer."

And indeed, the myriad requirements for the Seed Box loomed worse than I, ever the optimist, had imagined.

As the deadline approached, I began to moan to my family. "We have to pick an area of study; I think I'll choose *Radio*. Then she wants an original, illustrated story, weeks of lesson plans, diagrams of classroom posters, a booklet with scientific facts, original drawings of our proposed subject, test papers for students, suggested interviews with experts ... "

The list went on. "I can't do it," I said. "I'm no good at drawing or posters. I can write, but that's about it."

To my surprise, Art spoke up. "I'm pretty good at mechanical drawings," he said. "I can certainly draw a radio. I'd be glad to help."

After that, literally for weeks, Art and I jointly fulfilled the horrible requirements of the Seed Box. He'd been an engineer and a Commander in the Navy. Art knew how to draw. Beautifully. I knew how to write.

Together, we fulfilled the overwhelming requirements of the project ... and together we received an "A+."

Now, fifty years and three household moves later, I still have the Seed Box. It was such an arduous project, and in the end such a Mt. Everest conquest, I haven't the heart to throw it away.

SOON AFTER GRADUATION, I WAS HIRED AS A PERMANENT TEACHER at a San Fernando Valley school. I'd love to say I was a great First Grade teacher.

Except I wasn't.

It took awhile before I figured out where I'd gone wrong.

CHAPTER TEN

The Rotten Apple Syndrome

It became obvious fairly soon; I was too tall to teach First Grade. For me, those little people were miles away, practically on the floor. I kept thinking to myself as I scanned the room, then searched ever lower, *Where ARE they?*

But that wasn't my only problem: as a stubborn German, willing to persist at a task until I got it right, I had no patience for tiny wigglers with ten-minute attention spans. Excellent teachers in that category were always quick with new and stimulating distractions to keep their pupils engaged.

Invariably, I lost the attention of my little people three times within the first hour. The one kiddie trick I learned was only a momentary cure. When I said sweetly, "Tricia is sitting up so nice and straight," every little person squirmed until they'd all achieved perfect posture in their chairs. Beyond that, I was hopeless.

Fortunately, I had a perceptive principal who grasped that even an initial failure might not be a total loss. Within the first semester she transferred me to Fifth Grade ... where, at last, I prospered.

And then something happened that briefly transformed our Woodland Hills Elementary school.

A new teacher, a back-biter, came on board to teach Third Grade. Immediately she began an underhanded campaign which soon turned treacherous. Day after day she whispered to other teachers in the break room ... "Did you hear what our principal said today?" "Did you notice what Mrs. Semerenko did?" "Have you heard the latest from our fearless leader?" "I can't *believe* she's so inept."

Then "inept" became "clueless" and finally "disgusting." Before long most of us turned sour, even began to actively dislike the woman in charge.

It was my first acquaintance with the rotten-apple syndrome. By herself this one malcontent had altered the dynamics of our faculty. I'd never seen such a change; among us discontent, even rebellion, now reigned.

To her credit, Mrs. Semerenko eventually caught on to the problem … and better yet, she figured out who was causing it. Suddenly Mrs. Evil wasn't there anymore.

No explanation was ever offered—but like magic, our attitudes slowly reverted, and soon enough we were all as supportive of our principal as we'd been before.

That incident was a stark lesson in how profoundly a single rotten apple can affect the whole barrel. For me, it pointed to the amazing ability of one sinister individual to undermine the good will of everyone around her.

For the first time I vaguely understood how Hitler rose to power.

EARLY IN MY TEACHING CAREER, THE BOUNDARIES OF OUR LITTLE tract house became too tight, nearly unbearable. Anxiously, but with limited funds, Rob and I cast about for a larger home. Farther into the San Fernando Valley, Woodland Hills, in fact, we found an ideal house. On a street called Winnetka, the place came with what seemed a luxurious half acre of land. Rob's increased salary at Liberty Mutual made a mortgage affordable—if only we could scrape up a down payment.

Since my grandfather, Russell, was no longer with us, we explored the problem with my father, now living on Long Island in an even bigger house, once featured in *House Beautiful*. Because his second family of four kids all called him Ted, I did too.

"Ted's going to loan us the money!" I yelled as I got off the phone. "We can buy that house!"

"Twenty-five hundred feet," said Rob. "Three times what we have now. I suspect it'll be big enough ... maybe indefinitely."

"Bigger than I ever dreamed," I said as I wandered from the playroom, to the oversize kitchen, then to the expansive living room and nearby den. "I can't believe this will all be ours."

"Believe it, Babe," he said. "Just believe it."

And then Rob bought our first television—a wonder in black and white, with a screen that was tiny by today's standards. Though other families had already made this gigantic leap, we were mesmerized that we could sit in our den and actually "go to the movies."

During my second year of teaching, I began experiencing a kind of schizophrenia, a feeling that I'd become two people, neither connected to the other.

In school I was a respected teacher ... though with one glaring deficiency: I was such a dunce at math it took me hours each month-end Friday to reconcile my attendance records. Long after everyone else had gone home, I'd be fretting over figures that simply wouldn't "balance."

Still, I loved my students, loved sharing what I knew of literature, history, and science. I was enchanted that these fifth-graders seemed to care what I said, that they actually listened. At Christmas I formed a choir and taught them, by ear, to sing in harmony ... exactly as my mother had once taught me. One December day, to their delight, we performed for the whole school.

But on my drive home each day I could feel myself becoming someone else ... a mother.

Once at home all thoughts of school vanished; I was swept into the care of Rob and three sons ... almost as though the school didn't exist. Which meant that on my own turf I seldom managed to attack school chores ... like grading papers or preparing lesson plans.

As a teacher I was too often "winging it."

One evening I shared with Rob. "Sometimes I feel incompetent at school. I don't change the bulletin boards, and I never grade papers at home

… or even think about lesson plans. I'm too busy being a mother. These days I'm not sure who I really am."

He gave me a thoughtful look. "I've gotta guess you're not the only one. Ask around. See how many teachers have kids at home."

"Only two," I said. "With one child each."

"Hmm. Just do the best you can, Babe."

His non answer was little comfort—but at least he'd listened.

Sometime later, after we'd spent many months in what seemed our permanent home, our world changed again. In late '55, without Rob's knowledge, L. Dale Coffman, dean of the UCLA law school, gave Rob a strong positive recommendation for a job as sole attorney for Petrolane, a corporation in Long Beach.

Rob went for the interview, and came home smiling. "I got the job, Babe! It's mine!" Suddenly our salary had tripled, and now the family had excellent health insurance and even a new car.

However, his new role came with a serious drawback: Long Beach was a distant city. Though Rob briefly tried to commute, he soon said, "Can't do it, Babe. It takes me two hours each way. I'll have to live there during the week."

At my look of dismay, he said, "Don't worry. I'll be home weekends. We can get by."

My optimism came roaring back. "I guess we'll manage," I said. But with Rob gone most days, I had to hire help—a wonderful woman named "Pepper." Pepper took over, and all at once I found time for things I hadn't done before—like taking two of our kids for a walk.

But some things never changed. Always the worrywart about the possibility of someone choking, I warned Pepper constantly about leaving small objects around, lest our baby put in his mouth something that could cause a disaster. Clearly, the older children were listening.

One Friday, Bobby, Chris and I were off to the park. We hadn't gone far when a terrier came loping up, carrying a tennis ball in its mouth.

As Bobby approached him, the dog just stood there. Across Bobby's face came a look of concern. Leaning close, he reached out for the drippy white object and spoke into the animal's face. "Give me that ball. You might choke yourself, honey."

For a short while, life in that new house was wonderful. But our halcyon days didn't last. And we couldn't entirely blame the house.

CHAPTER ELEVEN

A Mixed Bag at Winnetka

As much as we loved our new, spacious home in Woodland Hills, the two of us wondered, in retrospect, if the place came with a run of bad karma.

It all began within months of our moving in.

Surely we couldn't have anticipated that at two in the morning an out-of-control car would come barreling down our nearby curvy hill, that it would cross our generous lawn and crash into the front bedroom.

Simultaneously we heard it and felt it. A sudden, thunderous jolt. A bomb against the house?

Rob and I were blasted awake. "What!! What!" I screamed.

"An earthquake!" cried Rob.

He listened hard. "Not an earthquake," he said, "something else."

The two of us leaped out of bed and explored the house. And there it was, the nose of a car jutting into the bedroom where two of our children had been fast asleep. A strange light gleamed off the car's hood.

Luckily, neither bed was placed along that wall.

Chris and Eric sat up, surprised and yawning. Seeing they were okay, the two of us ran outside to view the car and driver.

But the car was there by itself. Whoever had been at the wheel … well, he wasn't there now.

We kept looking; the driver had obviously run away. Yet he'd been out of control for quite a while, traveled a long distance from the road, and left a deep track across the grass.

I'm not sure we ever learned the identity of the mystery house-crasher. We asked the police, but they couldn't tell us anything. Instead we kept guessing: a stolen car, maybe? A joyrider?

"That person must have been drinking," I said. "Look how far he came!"

Within a week our insurance company arranged to patch up the bedroom. One of the workers remarked, "It's lucky you have such a good, solid house."

IT WAS AFTER ROB BEGAN WORKING IN LONG BEACH THAT WE HAD our second trauma. It must have been summer, because the accident happened midday when I was alone with my children. I had just returned from the grocery store. "I can carry that big sack," Bobby said, and hefted it into his arms and started for the house.

Leaving the side door open, he made it half way across our vast playroom when the sack gave way and a bottle of grape juice crashed to the floor—onto thin linoleum laid over cement. With that, Bobby slipped in the juice and fell on a chunk of glass.

When I ran into the room, I found him standing over the mess and bleeding. He was shocked, but not crying. "I've got a pretty bad cut," he said.

Horrified, I examined the knee and saw that the flesh, white underneath, had parted clear to the bone. I've never forgiven myself for what I did next. Instead of helping my son to a seat, I was so terrified I left him standing and raced into the next room to phone a doctor.

When I returned, a concerned neighbor, Delores, was there. She must have heard the commotion through the open door. Now in our playroom, she'd helped Bobby to a chair and placed a cloth over the damaged knee.

"Oh, thank you! Thank you!" I cried. "What would I have done without you?"

From that moment on, I vowed never again to react so badly to an emergency.

IT MUST HAVE BEEN DELORES WHO ARRANGED FOR A BABY-SITTER, then drove us to the hospital.

Rob rushed home from Long Beach to find Bobby in surgery and me in a nearby waiting room. Rob didn't take it well. "How do we know he'll ever be able to walk again?" he growled. "How in hell did this happen?"

Later we realized that a grocery checker had packed a head of wet lettuce in the same sack as the grape juice, thereby weakening the paper so the grape juice fell out.

When Bobby returned home two days later, he had a cast the entire length of his leg. The doctor told us that the quadriceps tendon had been severed. "But it's now securely stitched," he said. "It will take some time to heal—but he's young, and I expect him to heal fast." He gave us a reassuring nod. "Take heart. If he's careful with that leg, he'll soon be able to walk again."

But Bobby, being Bobby, didn't wait for nature to perform its miracle. Instead, whenever he felt like moving, he scooted across the floor until he wore a hole in the cast. Sooner than anyone expected, we had to take him back for a new one. Eventually our son wore out three casts on his way to recovery.

One day when I was once again alone with our kids, I put Bobby on a wagon and took the three kids to a park. But I soon noticed other parents shaking their heads and giving me looks of pity. Here I was, a lady walking slowly with a child encased in a long cast and two younger children trailing along beside her.

I couldn't endure looking so pathetic. That was our last such excursion while we lived in that house.

IN LATE 1955, OUR LIVES ONCE AGAIN CHANGED: TO MY SURPRISE, EVEN dismay, I realized I was once again pregnant.

"Can't be," said Rob. "This time it really can't be."

"But I know the symptoms, Rob. I don't need a test. The signs are unmistakable. I wish it wasn't true. But it is."

He kept shaking his head. "We've been so careful. Are you sure?"

"Too sure."

Finally he said, "Well, we'll adjust, Babe. It'll be okay."

RUTH'S REACTION TO THE NEWS WILL REMAIN FOREVER FIXED IN memory. One afternoon when she was visiting and about to leave, I said, "Ruth, I have something to tell you."

"Yes?"

I paused. "We're going to have another baby."

Abruptly she stopped short. The oldest of seven children herself, she turned and stared at me. Her face transformed into a look of horror. Then she began to scream. "No! Oh, no! No! No! No!" Turning away, she ran out of the house, still screaming. I could hear her cries reaching me from out on the street.

I stood in the kitchen, transfixed. Or more, frozen. In spite of her frequent emotionalism, I'd never encountered anything close to this … nothing so fraught with anguish.

In silence, my feelings did a similar spin—from surprise, to dismay, and finally to anger. She'd demeaned us both, and I would never forget that moment. No longer could I entirely trust her.

WHEN, IN THE FALL OF 1955, I RETURNED TO THE CLASSROOM, MY teaching became a test of willpower. Extreme nausea does not work well with a room full of students. I could no longer stand in front of the class, but instead sat in a chair, comforting myself by swinging one leg or the other back and forth.

I can't throw up, I kept telling myself. *I must control this awful feeling.*

But as usual, even nibbling on crackers did little to calm the roiling waves—and worse, I wasn't giving my students my full attention. When you're sick, you're sick. Internal disruptions tend to blot out everything.

By Christmas it was clear I had to quit.

WITH THREE KIDS AND ANOTHER ON THE WAY, IT WAS OBVIOUS MY teaching days were over. I would now be a full-time mother.

About February, when I was six months along and wickedly pregnant, I somehow caught the mumps. Though my obstetrician assured me the disease would not affect the baby, it certainly affected me. Here I was, swollen above and swollen below.

My jaw was so huge that it affected the salivary glands, which abruptly stopped functioning. My saliva disappeared and I could no longer swallow anything without help. I literally washed down each bite with a gulp of water.

As I might have done at a freak show, I stared at myself in the mirror. This was no longer me, it was a grotesque version of me, barely recognizable.

Assured by the doctor that both the baby and I would recover, at times I almost thought it funny. I said to Rob, "You'll never see anything like this again. A hugely pregnant lady with the mumps."

"Somehow, Babe, I don't see the humor in this. Hurry up and get well, will you?"

"I'm hurrying, Rob. I'm hurrying! But I'd sure like to get my saliva back. Eating is nearly impossible."

It seemed like forever, but long before my due date the jaw returned to normal.

ON JUNE 8, 1956, ROB AND I WERE ONCE MORE SURPRISED. IT WAS MY obstetrician who delivered both the baby and the news. "Mrs. Wills," he said warmly, "you have a fine baby boy."

I just looked at him. *Why are you acting so pleased? Over yet another boy?*

I thought our doctor was heartless, that he should have known better and apologized.

Only later did I discover that he wasn't so heartless after all. Through a complicated grapevine I learned that my doctor, earlier that day, had said to another of his patients, "I've got to go tell a woman she's just had her fourth boy."

BACK HOME WITH OUR NEW BABY, IT WAS MY OTHER CHILDREN WHO made me fully appreciate baby Kenny. While they crowded around, I laid him on the couch in the den. "Look at his toes!" Chris said, carefully touching his foot. "He's so tiny. And so perfect."

"Yeah, look at him!" said Eric. "He's really cute."

Well, I thought, *maybe a fourth boy will do just fine.*

CHAPTER TWELVE

Orange County, Here we Come

OUR BIG NEW HOUSE, FOR ALL ITS LOVELINESS, LEFT US WITH A CRUEL parting blow. Thanks to the property's grove of walnut trees which filled the backyard, that first spring when the trees bloomed, Bobby began coughing. Rob and I had no idea what had brought this on.

That summer, when the blooms disappeared, so did his coughing. The second summer, Bobby's response to the pollen lingered. At night we could hear him wheezing. By the time we left that house, Bobby was diagnosed as a serious asthmatic.

Since we hadn't caught on by then to the walnut tree problem, our leaving was propelled by common sense. Rob's Long Beach job had split the family for too long. His job as the sole in-house attorney for a large corporation called Petrolane gave him a generous salary, but its location made our present home impractical. Rob's week nights in a distant rented room weren't exactly great, either.

The obvious next step was to research homes in Long Beach.

But that's not how our choice was made.

In a strange irony, our family's selection of a new location came about because of "San Fernando Valley" friends of Rob's parents, Bill and Dorothy Pruner (a lively couple, closer in age to us than them). The two had already purchased a home elsewhere, and one day Bill offered to lead us to his new, rustic community called Tustin.

"*Tustin?*" I said, with no enthusiasm. "What kind of name is that?"

"You'll see," said Bill Pruner. "Besides, the town has the world's best burger joint. *Kenny's Cheeseburgers.* Wanna come try 'em?"

Like Hansel and Gretel's bread crumbs, the cheeseburgers led us to Bill's drowsy community with the weird name. But beyond the burgers, which lived up to their billing, the community itself sucked us in. The neighborhoods were only sporadically developed with a few clusters of homes … an area largely occupied by the dark-green hue of orange groves. Tustin's main boulevard, 17th Street, marched West to East, proudly display-ing its best feature, a dividing strip of stately eucalyptus trees.

In every way, Tustin resembled the San Fernando Valley when we first arrived, though instead of cows being the predominant feature, here orange groves outnumbered the homes.

Although Tustin was still a half-hour's drive from Long Beach, we'd found the kind of community we'd long cherished: a homey area with scant traffic and, in some areas, large country lots.

That first year—1956—we moved into a newly-built ranch-style house on a street called Bikini, whose three bedrooms, convenient kitchen (with my first, ever, dishwasher), and 1800 square feet seemed better than just adequate. Though the lot was small, the house had both a living and family room. Best of all, the elementary school was only a few blocks away, mean-ing Bobby, and later Chris, were able to walk.

For me, memories of that house are tied to one of my most embar-rassing moments. In those days, men chosen for their affable personalities delivered milk right to our homes. Sometimes, after a brief knock, they sim-ply walked in to deposit bottles in the refrigerator. One of those mornings I heard the back door open (no knock), recognized the approaching footsteps of the Arden man, and realized we were both in for a nasty surprise.

Unhappily, I was in the kitchen, naked—and in a part of the room from which I couldn't escape except by streaking right past the milkman. Horrified, and knowing I was trapped, for seconds I saw no way to cover up. Then suddenly it came to me. With desperate speed, I squatted down and pulled open the nearest cupboard door, which shielded at least parts of me. He came in, all right, deposited his bottles and retreated. I hardly breathed until he left.

Whether the milkman noticed me there, squatting and hiding, I'll never know. I was a 5'10" woman, crouching behind a 3' cabinet door. He probably spotted me, all right, and chose to pretend he didn't. In any case, that episode makes the house forever lodged in memory.

WHEN, TWO YEARS LATER, WE FINALLY MOVED AWAY, WE KEPT THE place as a rental. While we had a series of good tenants (most of whom became friends), for various reasons families never seemed to stay longer than a year, meaning that each summer I was forced to drive over to Bikini and re-paint, mow the lawn, and water the plants. It got to be a drag.

When we finally sold it, some seven years later, we found property values had scarcely changed, so those years had not been profitable.

On the other hand, the house eventually acquired a reputation. Years later, we became friends with an infectious disease specialist and his wife, who lived there long after we left. Somewhere in that time frame the house became famous for the worst possible reason. A tragedy.

After school, the young son of one of its families was murdered. The parents came home from work to find him slashed and dead in the kitchen—his assailant unknown— and even long after, a killer who escaped apprehension.

The family never slept there again. That day the remaining members moved out and never returned.

AFTER THOSE TWO YEARS AT BIKINI, WE WERE ABLE, FOR $7000, TO purchase a half-acre from a dentist and build the home we'd always wanted. As we showed the lot to our boys, Chris and Bobby were ecstatic. "Look, Eric, we've got an orange grove!" Clearly, our property on Beverly Glen more than met their approval.

We chose among the community's three most highly recommended builders to erect a 2500-square-foot house. The design itself we selected from a *Los Angeles Times* catalog—one architect's home plans and schematics—a decision we never regretted.

It was young Glenn Burrus, a foreman for the Nelson Company, who did all the framing and most of the subcontracting ... and Burrus himself who, over the years, "added on" here and there until our house grew to 4400 square feet. Just this year, in 2017, Burrus finally retired, at age 90—a consummate builder to the end.

BY THE TIME OUR HOUSE BEGAN GOING UP, I WAS—SURPRISE— ONCE again pregnant. And yes, for us, the cost of the new project became significant. For a reduced bill, I offered to take over the entire job of painting.

Annoyed by my growing protuberance, I painted window frames galore, the kind of tedious work no painter relishes. On and on I painted, two coats of white on all the tiny edges, which must have outlined a thousand small panes of glass.

"I can't do this any more," I groaned to Rob as I finished the last window. So he bought back the contract—at which point professional painters came in with great, efficient, free-flowing rollers, and painted all the rooms.

"They did the easy part," I said. "I wish I'd started with the rooms and let *them* paint the window frames."

My last effort on the house was the planting of a front-yard tree. Bending over, with my huge stomach seriously in the way, I was just digging the hole when my water broke.

Rob was out of town, so neighbors watched the kids while my current babysitter rushed me to the hospital.

As I walked in the entrance, leaving behind a noticeable trail, somebody popped me into a wheelchair, and away I went to the obstetrical area.

From then on, everything about the delivery was different, almost a breeze. This time, instead of steadily-escalating pain, I had pain-free moments when I could relax and revive. *So this is how labor contractions are supposed to be*, I thought.

84

To top it off, the baby arrived quickly—probably within a few hours. By early afternoon it was over, and the doctor was ebullient. "You have a girl!" he exclaimed.

"What?" I cried. "A girl? Are you serious?"

"Here she is!" and he plopped her onto my stomach.

That became one of the biggest moments of my life. Rob called from Bakersfield and found me virtually trembling with excitement. "Our baby's a girl!" I shouted. "We have a girl!" That night the excitement remained so intense that one sleeping pill, then another, failed to induce sleep.

No drug, it seemed, was strong enough to dim the thrill of finding ourselves, so unexpectedly, with a sweet baby daughter.

Our new friends in the Tustin area were equally impressed. For months the little-girl gifts kept coming, as though part of a never-ending celebration.

UNLIKE THE OTHER HOMES ON OUR STREET, WE CHOSE OUR DESIGN partly because most of the important windows—family room and kitchen—faced our generous back yard. Knowing my command post would be the kitchen sink, that I'd be practically nailed there, I relished the arrangement—that I could so easily do dishes and watch the kids.

And watch them I did. What I didn't actually *see* out in the play area, I almost always *heard*.

One day an argument erupted between Bobby and Eric, resulting in some kind of lashing out from Bobby. A rather skimpy fight, at best. Still, I heard Eric cry out indignantly, "I'm going to tell Mother on you!" With that, he whirled around and headed for the house. *Here he comes*, I thought.

And sure enough, seconds later Eric was in the kitchen, pouring out his grievances against Bobby. Since they seemed relatively minor, I listened with half an ear, making only a quick, offhanded comment. Which, for some reason, seemed to satisfy my aggrieved son, who then quickly departed.

Moments later I heard them again as Eric returned to the scene, newly wrapped in triumph. He marched up to Bobby and declared, "I told Mother on you!"

"Yeah?" Bobby asked. "What did she say?"

To my surprise, Eric solemnly delivered the truth. "She said 'Oh!'"

Strangely, that finished it for both of them.

I tried not to laugh so the kids could hear me.

As it turned out, we'd moved into a neighborhood that was busily constructing a tennis club. Owned entirely by the "life members" in our neighborhood, we, one of the rare monthly subscribers, eventually found ourselves within a half mile of three swimming pools and two tennis courts.

From the moment the club opened, our lives veered off in directions we'd never anticipated. Within a short time, our three older boys learned to swim.

But then down came a hammer.

"Your kids can't come up here and just *swim*," various mothers informed me. "They can't hang around and play. We need them for our swim team. You've got enough boys for every age group!"

"Really?" I was surprised. "But they don't know any competitive strokes. They're just dog-paddling."

"Don't worry about trivial stuff like that," Nancy G. said. She was one of the two pushiest mothers. "Our coach will teach them. Think how exciting this will be—watching your kids compete!"

"I'm not sure about any of this," I said. "I'm pretty busy at home."

"Never mind *Busy at Home*. We need your kids. You've got to sign them up."

"Well ..."

"No 'wells' allowed. Here's the application form."

And so it happened. Our three older boys had been conscripted like soldiers for a juvenile army. Our local recreational pool had evolved into serious business, organized and overseen by a group of martinet mothers. For about ten years they more or less ran our lives.

And it wasn't all bad.

CHAPTER THIRTEEN

Moving Like An Inchworm

When Tracy was only four months old, I was given a rare medical opportunity. I'd long coped with outrageously large bunions—which, when they weren't hurting, stretched and distorted my shoes. The pain was infrequent but obnoxious—but even more, I hated how my feet looked and anguished over the difficulty of finding comfortable shoes.

One day my father, with his physician's network, told me about Dr. Joplin, a colleague from Boston who'd developed as his specialty a surgery that rearranged his patients' foot and ankle tendons and left the foot bunion-free. Dr. Joplin was planning a trip to Orange County to demonstrate The Joplin Procedure, and my Dad suggested I'd be a perfect candidate. "Dr. Joplin's qualifications are impeccable," he said.

I quickly agreed. I'd lived with those irritating feet long enough. Though I was still nursing Tracy, I recognized Joplin's visit as a once-in-a-lifetime chance to escape an irksome part of my anatomy.

Not knowing what to expect, I was surprised by two elements: One, I was awake throughout the event, and two, the operating room was packed with local surgeons, all circling my bed. In a strange way, I'd become a sort of *Star Among Patients,* reveling in attention I'd never received as a bride (married with no fanfare by a San Jose Justice of the Peace.)

Well, I thought, *it's kind of nice after all, being the queen.*

With that, the pounding and sawing began. I felt nothing except for moments of "stretching." The surgery involved removal of the bunion and an adjustment of tendons so my ankle muscles would pull in new directions, eliminating any chance the bunions would return. The circling surgeons seemed impressed.

Afterwards—with hospital stays considerably longer back then—I remained confined for about a week. Meanwhile, I was told by the local surgeon, "You do understand, Maralys, that you can't walk at all for three months." It took a while to fully absorb what that meant.

Since I wanted to continue nursing, our baby-sitter brought Tracy to the hospital midday, and Rob brought her at night. The difference couldn't have been greater. At noon the baby-sitter did herself proud. Tracy arrived in a pretty little dress, clean diapers, attractive socks, and nicely wrapped in a blanket.

Her late-night visit suggested she was homeless. If she was dressed at all, her clothes were hastily assembled, her diaper in need of a change, the blanket thrown around her so carelessly she resembled a bundle of rags. "You're just lucky I can make it at all," Rob said. "You forget I work in Long Beach."

I remembered, all right; just looking at Tracy reminded me.

Once home again, the no-walking dictum changed our family's lives. I couldn't stand, so I had to scoot around on the floor, moving like an inch-worm—backwards. I'd draw in my legs, then lift with my arms and push my rear along. My movements were both unattractive and exceedingly slow.

It was quickly obvious my five children needed someone with legs.

Though we never asked him, seven-year-old Chris slipped into that role. Each school day he awakened his brothers, made sure they were adequately dressed, then came to the kitchen to make breakfast—which in those days consisted of an eggnog … eggs, powdered skim milk, and chocolate Quick, beat to a froth in our blender.

I sat on the floor and watched. "Chris, you're doing everything just right," I said. To me, he was a miracle.

Chris grinned. "Not much to it," he said.

But there was much to it.

How did he know, with Rob a late sleeper, that only he was capable of taking over? That only he had that inner sense of leadership?

With quiet efficiency, those week-days, Chris made sure his brothers had shoes, breakfast, and lunch money, then he herded them out the door.

With only a dim memory of that period, I suspect Rob brought in dinners. Or perhaps we had a baby-sitter who arrived later.

At night, when Tracy awoke, crying for a bottle, Chris (again without being asked), woke up and brought her one. For three months he was our leader, taking over with no fanfare. Even now I can hardly believe he was only seven.

At last one day the three month walking hiatus was over. How well I remember that moment in the kitchen when I first stood. Slowly I rose to my feet, and like Alice in Wonderland, I seemed to grow and grow, higher and higher until I stood looking DOWN at the drainboard—which for months I'd only seen from below. For several astonishing minutes I felt like a newly-created giant.

The sensation was unforgettable. And my new feet were as straight and bunion-free as I'd hoped.

At last Chris could revert to being a child. Yet one night, soon after I was walking again, I woke up in the middle of the night because I heard Tracy crying. As I headed down the hall, I found Chris coming the other way. And he was carrying a bottle.

When, in later years, he became an orthopedic surgeon, those same caring traits served him well.

Chapter Fourteen

A Frenetic Stolen Summer

When we first moved in to our newly-built house, the kids considered the orange groves lining the back of the lot to be a divine feature. For them, the groves became a kind of personal theme park. It was there they could give full rein to their imaginations or their bellicose natures, whichever came first.

With no sense that they were in danger, I let my kids roam, guessing they wouldn't go far.

A grove with a plentiful supply of hanging oranges was all the inducement young males needed—though the group was eventually augmented by our daughter, Tracy … and later by other warriors, friends of both sexes.

What could be more exciting than free access to ongoing orange wars—juicier and more entertaining than snowball fights. Only vaguely did I grasp what was going on—learning long after the groves were gone the extent of our kids' enjoyment. "We hid behind the trees and splatted each other with the juiciest oranges. We had a blast!" Bobby confessed.

In those early Tustin days Rob and I attached more activities to the Wills kids than orange fights and swim meets … add-ons to our lives and theirs, numerous in the extreme. Like our contemporaries, we parents all thought our children required lessons—instruction in just about everything. And especially during the summer months, when they needed to be "occupied." Thus, we added music to their schedules, additional sports, and in late June, church school.

"Kids need to be busy," we kept hearing—but then one summer the "busy-ness" erupted until it was out of control. Those were a couple of months I'll never forget.

Not only did each child participate in one or more sports—swimming, tennis, or baseball—but Bobby took piano lessons and Chris and Eric were tutored on the trumpet. And then our Presbyterian Church persuaded me to enroll them in summer church school. And I, now in the church choir, was designated to be one of the teachers.

How well I recall my older three boys shuffling down the church sidewalk behind me, feet dragging as though heading for jail. In later discussions, Chris remarked unpleasantly, "That damn program lasted for months."

"Not really, Chris. It was only three weeks."

"Well, it seemed like months."

ENDLESS CHURCH SCHOOL OR NOT, THAT SUMMER STANDS OUT AS ghastly. Unable to remember which child was to appear where and for what activity, I had to keep a schedule posted on the refrigerator. The logistical details would have challenged an astronaut. All day long, each hour of every day, I was committed to driving one or another to an activity, while picking up someone else who was finished. Somehow, meals were part of the rat race.

Never have a few hot months been more disagreeable—both for me and my children. I vowed I'd never let myself organize another summer like it. And I didn't.

Someone should have mentioned a long recognized adage about childhood: *Children need free time ... to play creatively ... to dream ... to think.*

And so do moms.

Chapter Fifteen

The Shopworn Shoebox

EVENTUALLY THAT AWFUL SUMMER RAT RACE BECAME FALL, AND with it our kids' return to school. Kenny was now in second grade, and soon Tracy would start kindergarten. Our sixth and newest baby, Kirk, (born a year and a half after Tracy), was eligible for preschool.

For awhile I was free to pursue a life-long passion: writing.

I began my career in typical writerly fashion: I typed and mailed out poems, short stories, essays, humorous tidbits … researching all the available markets, paying attention to such requirements as word length and the famous SASE (self-addressed stamped envelope.)

At times, with a helper, Dell, who was almost a member of the family, and mostly during the dinner hour (because there's no better time to escape), I went down to Kirk's pre-school, the Little Red School House near our church. Using a borrowed key, and carrying my typewriter, I parked at the teacher's desk and worked madly for a few hours, enjoying the luxury of no kids and no phone.

With monotonous—and of course disappointing—precision, everything I'd written came winging back.

I saved every rejection. Not because I'm a masochist, but because I had blind faith in my eventual success: For me, getting published was never a matter of "IF," only "WHEN." *How many Nos will it take,* I wondered, *before I ever get a Yes?* All my rejections went into a rumpled shoebox, to be counted when that magic day arrived. I planned to give speeches and, with my audience paying rapt attention, dramatically dump the contents of my box on the floor.

Until you get paid, I told myself, *you're not a writer: you're just a mother with a typewriter.*

I never dreamed it would take so long.

Finally I began writing a book, *Rough Around the Edges.* Now in communication with my father, still living on Long Island, but working in New York, I began forwarding chapters of what I considered a humorous tale. I thought my stuff was quite funny.

He didn't. And neither did any of his associates. But he imparted his criticisms gently, with both admiration and advice. He said, "Why don't you read Betty McDonald's *Onions in the Stew?* She has done successfully what you're trying to do."

With his advice ringing in my head, I did more than *read* McDonald's book. I studied it. Sentence by sentence. Episode by episode … developing a sense of how humor is transmitted, how exaggeration and cleverness are woven in to everyday episodes. I began to see that pretence is part of the technique, that an author's view of craziness means she pretends that everything on the page is *normal,* while the reader realizes the episode is anything but.

I discovered that some words are just naturally funnier than others. I learned about the use of the unexpected verb, the surprise at the end, the element of "call back" which means the story finishes with a reference to something outrageous mentioned earlier.

Gradually, with analysis and obsessive re-writes my work became better. My father and his friends began saying that they now found themselves laughing.

I hadn't yet sold anything, but I'd developed an audience, albeit a few readers on the other side of the continent.

Little did I know that 30 years later parts of this story would become chapters of a published book, *A Circus Without Elephants.*

When chris, and then Bobby, now in their mid to late teens, began hang gliding, I wrote stories about them, carefully maintaining the fiction that they were someone else's sons.

Quite soon a photographer friend became part of my efforts, providing me with photos. How well I remember the package I sent to *United Airlines Mainliner Magazine.*

As always, weeks later I heard from them. But this time it wasn't the return of my article. Instead, I found a letter with a check inside. They'd enclosed $350—enough for a ticket to Hawaii. I whooped and shouted.

I now considered myself an *author*. Because I quickly sold other articles about this amazing new sport, I imagined my days of rejection were over.

I'm glad I didn't know, then, that the 129 rejections residing in the now-dilapidated shoe box were a mere down payment on a writing career.

With my father involved long-distance and intent on helping me, I began learning more about HIM. Not only was he an excellent writer himself, but his background story was amazing, worthy of a novel.

In later years, my granddaughter, Christy, did the research on Theodore George Klumpp and brought me the facts. From them I've written the story as I imagined it to be. The next chapter is all about my father, "Ted."

Chapter Sixteen

The Two Doctors Klumpp

Stuttgart, Germany. February 8, 1869.

For a cold evening in the wooded section of Stuttgart, the German wedding had an unusual aura of warmth and good cheer. Outside, the falling snow was quiet, relentless. But inside the biergarten—all stone and brick—the yellow-painted walls reflected back the heat of the revelers. Above their heads, alpine horns, antlered elk heads and multi-colored local flags lined the walls, adding to an air of festivity.

Surrounded by male friends, Christian Ludwig Heinrich Klumpp raised his beer stein to salute them. "Ach! I will soon lose my freedom!" he sang out, but one of them shouted back, "Jah! But you vill once more test your manhood!" and with that, the group roared.

Nearby, Margaretha Schnieder, sheltered within a cluster of women attendants, blushed in chagrin. So it was known everywhere then-—that Heinrich had once spread his masculinity throughout the village.

With the eyes of the revelers upon her, Margaretha straightened proudly. *He is mine,* she thought, *and all his carousing is now over.* She patted the skirt of her white, batiste gown. *From this day forward, Heinrich will not dare be found in any bed but mine.*

Outside, the church bells rang, casting solemn notes into the icy February air. Soon accordion music from within the beer garden seeped out through cracks around the window and joined the church bells in song. A wedding was always a fine reason to combine one kind of note with another.

THE KNOCK ON MARGARETHA'S DOOR, MONTHS LATER, SEEMED innocent enough, though wholly unexpected. Heavy with child, she responded calmly to the midday tap on her oaken door, surprised to see the woman who stood outside. The fraulein's black hair was pulled straight back, and her face, clearly once comely, was now a mask of fatigue combined with stolid German determination. A small boy in short pants stood at her side.

"Yes?" Margaretha asked.

The woman didn't hesitate. Lifting the boy's arm, she said, "This is my child, Karl—the son of Heinrich. An unexpected event ... so it's likely Heinrich does not know. But see? He's the image of your husband."

"You and ... Heinrich?" Margaretha stared down at the child, the shock registering on her face, turning her pale.

"I am Rosina Wagner. Without money, I cannot continue to raise him."

"You are asking for money? But Heinrich doesn't have—"

"I want no money. For myself, I scrub houses, I am fed. But the boy here is too large, three years old, he can no longer come with me to each workplace. You must take him. You and Heinrich. He's yours now." Abruptly, she pulled the child's hand from her own.

"Mine?" The other gasped. "I am already with child."

"So I see. You will now have another for company." Rosina bent down to kiss her son. "Be good, Karl. Good-bye."

Before Margaretha could catch her breath, Rosina had straightened and was striding rapidly away, with Karl looking after her, masking a sob.

For long seconds, while the boy's sobs became audible, Margaretha stood in shock. She was torn. *Mein Gott, this can't be. How did this happen? How am I to take another's child?* But then the boy's disconsolate crying tore at her. As he snuffled and gasped, Margaretha's heart broke.

Awkwardly, she leaned down. "Oh, poor child," she said. "Poor, poor boy. Come to me." With that she squatted and took the boy in her arms. "Sweet little tyke," she murmured into his hair. Above his shoulders she saw the looming trees, the darkness deep in the forest, expanding even beyond the obvious shadows. "We cannot leave you to the fearsome forest, can we? You will have a home." Against her rounded abdomen she rocked him briefly. "Oh, Karl. How shall we tell your father?"

BUT SHE DID ... AND THE YEARS THAT FOLLOWED DID NOT GO WELL for Karl. Joined by a half-sister, Marie, and later a half-brother, Gustav, he was treated by Heinrich as a nuisance—or worse, a pariah. "Get that child out of my sight," he said whenever he saw Karl.

"Be good to him," cried Margaretha time and again, "for he is your son, too. Ignore him and he will hate you."

His answer was always a stony stare. And then, "Not willingly mine, he's not. His mother brought him here to taunt me—that I married you instead of her. She had other lovers."

"He looks like you."

"Bah! What does that mean, woman? I do not accept him as mine."

"But you must." Karl was now almost five.

Even as he grew older and increasingly resembled his father, the boy seemed to attract only added paternal hostility.

At last Margaretha felt she must act. Karl had now turned fourteen.

Telling no one her plan, she began earning money, often secretly, then hiding most from her husband. From the finer households she took in sewing. Washed her neighbor's clothes. Served as a tutor, teaching children to read. On rare nights she handed over coins to Heinrich, but kept more for herself.

Within a year and a half she had managed the price of a boat passage to America. One day when Karl was still sixteen, she secretly and quickly packed a duffel with his clothes—garments that required minimum space, since he was full grown but only 5'6". She found them both a carriage ride to Hamburg.

With great sadness, she stood with him on the dock and pressed a roll of money into his hand. "I wish it was more," she said, and quickly kissed the youth she'd so lovingly raised as her own. "Be good, Karl," she whispered to him.

It was the second time in his life he'd heard the same admonition—the second time he'd been sent away. But this time the love that accompanied him formed a comforting shield against loneliness, a layer that warmed him and eased his departure.

In July, 1883, listed on the ship manifest, the *Selisia*, as a "joiner," in possession of only one bag, Karl became part of New York City's untamed, uncounted masses. With what ingenuity he managed to survive, even prosper, no record remains. Was he fed through the kindness of strangers? Given a job by dint of his youth and seventeen-year-old strength? Or did he simply find within himself the needed inspiration, bestowed so recently by a determined and loving stepmother?

Documents show that Karl Wagner Klumpp was naturalized on June 12, 1889, and when he applied for a passport in 1896 at the age of 29, he listed his occupation as "barber." In that 1896 application he wrote that he intended to go back to Germany and return "within one year."

Though it is not known how or where he found Marie Caroline Hayoz, eleven years his junior, surely it was a fortuitous encounter.

However they chanced to meet, one fact remains: they were married on December 5, 1897. And in time the two opened a bakery shop in the Bronx.

In may of 1903, my father, Theodore George, was born as the first child of Karl and Marie Klumpp, a birth that was followed three years later by that of a daughter.

My father seldom spoke to us about those growing-up years, when he and his one sister, Margaret, delivered fresh-baked bread to their parents' customers.

But the parents had loftier goals for their children than bread delivery: they managed somehow to send their son to Princeton and their daughter to Cornell.

Later I wished that somebody had recorded which parent—or was it both?—who inspired their two children to leave their humble Bronx backgrounds and enroll in two of the country's most elite universities.

BECAUSE THEODORE ENTERED PRINCETON'S FRESHMAN CLASS OF 1924 without the customary social credentials, neither wealthy nor a member of Eastern high society—and in spite of his obvious good looks—young Theodore Klumpp was never invited to join the prestigious Princeton Eating Club. Thus passed over, he said, "I'll form my own eating club," and so he did.

It was during those Princeton years that Theodore must have met my mother, Virginia Allan. When she brought "Ted" home to meet Russell Allan, her wealthy father, his approval was immediate. "He's graduating Magna Cum Laude," Virginia said. "And now he's been accepted to Harvard Medical school," which was all the prompting Russell needed. "Tell him to begin his medical education," said Russell. "And send the bills to me."

Thus did two amazing grandfathers converge to promote the career of one promising young man. For Russell it was an obvious decision to invest in a man whom he saw, correctly, as having a stellar future. Midway through his medical school education, according to the New York Times of February 14, 1926, Virginia Allan and Theodore Klumpp became engaged. The two were married later that year.

FOLLOWING HER BROTHER'S EXAMPLE, MARGARET KLUMPP, TOO, applied for admission to medical school. But she was told by the dean of Cornell, "I'm sorry, Miss Klumpp. This education would be wasted on you. You'll marry and have children and drop out. We cannot squander a classroom seat on a woman."

"But I won't drop out," she argued, "I give my word. No matter how my family life unfolds, I'll still continue my medical practice." With that promise taken at face value, she was accepted and became a dermatologist, one of the first female doctors in the United States. Keeping her word to the medical school—and in spite of an exceptionally good marriage to a businessman named Art Searing—she continued her dermatology practice for a lifetime.

Unfortunately, Margaret was unable to have children of her own, but instead she later became a loving aunt to her brother's children.

ONCE GRADUATED FROM HARVARD, DR. THEODORE KLUMPP DID HIS residency at the Peter Bent Brigham hospital in Boston, and was there when I was born. A short time later he was asked to teach medicine at Yale, and later at George Washington University.

Sadly, Karl Wagner Klumpp died in 1928, one year before his first grandchild was born. But he lived long enough to bask in the budding careers of his two children.

My father's teaching years ended in 1936, when he was tapped to become the chief medical officer for the Food and Drug Administration, a position he held until 1941. Passionate about the problems of aging and a strong proponent of exercise (not then a universally accepted mantra), he began writing articles on the subject, including some which were accepted by my beloved *Reader's Digest*.

Sometime during those years, after about five years of marriage, my mother divorced him. For my mother, we surmised, he fell short as a lover.

In 1942, Dr. Theodore George Klumpp was chosen by board members of Sterling Drug to become the CEO of Winthrop Laboratories in New York City.

With his new wife, also named Virginia, he built a home in Sands Point on Long Island, with its panoramic view of Long Island Sound. This was the house where, as an adult, I finally came to know my father—not as a kind of specter during a fleeting appearance on our ranch—nor later, when we shared a near-drowning at Jones beach, but now as a real person, a supportive adult.

Still, that week of our first in-depth acquaintance stands out as a transformative moment in my growing up. For the first time I learned what

I'd been missing all my growing-up years ... a loving father to envelop me in his arms and his affections.

The fact that he appeared, then disappeared (for what seemed like forever), left me, for months afterwards, a wounded child. Our re-acquaintance, through my efforts to become an author, was a kind of re-awakening.

As hard as I worked to become an author, for a number of years, thanks to our kids becoming steeped in sports, writing became almost a passing interest.

CHAPTER SEVENTEEN

The Sports Bonanza

As with other families, our lives became divided into distinctive segments, which at times felt disconnected from earlier or later eras.

Once our older children reached their teens and began driving, our contacts with a larger world began spreading outward, almost like a river overflowing its banks. Abruptly we were no longer chauffeuring the older ones to endless, diverse lessons, but instead we were *following them* as they headed in new directions ... to tennis and swimming competitions, and nearly simultaneously into a sport which, until then, we'd never heard of.

Our oldest son, Bobby, briefly went to college, but as he became obsessed with his own bizarre inventions out in the garage, he soon quit school. With an imagination that worked overtime, he was totally absorbed in what Rob and I considered a lot of time-wasting "fun:" Among his gadgets, he motorized the trash cart. "Anyone want to go for a ride?" he asked, and with siblings and their friends aboard, he put-putted down our cul-de-sac street. He produced, and then rode, a hill-climbing rototiller. Worst, for the neighbors, he created a go-cart that howled like a jet engine, ever louder as it accelerated.

But he also dreamed up a high-bike that had the rider ten feet in the air, which he subsequently rode down to his college, unaware that he was in full view of a Nobel prize winner's outdoor presentation. As Bobby crossed the man's line of vision, the speaker lost his train of thought and broke off, whereupon the college sent someone to chase Bobby away. For that, Bobby unwittingly made the local newspapers. "Cyclist Rides into Nobel Prize Winner's Speech."

Bobby's double-decker bicycle drew its own double-takes from nearby motorists—including a policeman, who alarmed Bobby into fearing he might get a ticket—though he wasn't sure what for. Instead, the cop stopped Bobby and his elevated pal to ask, "How do you get up on that thing?"

After the two descended, Bobby showed him. "I just give it a little push and climb up the tubes. Then my other rider jumps on."

To their relief, the patrolman said, "Thanks," and got back in his car and drove away.

FROM TIME TO TIME ROB GLARED AT THE MESS SPREAD OUT OVER the garage concrete ... at scattered tools, metal parts, and grease. "All he cares about," Rob groused, "are these Rube Goldbergs he keeps creating. Which will lead exactly nowhere."

Bobby either ignored his dad, or argued in return. "Some day one of these inventions will be important, Dad. You'll see."

Before that happened, Bobby was swept into Chris' dream of natural flight, and soon he became as skilled as Chris at flying bamboo and plastic hang gliders ... at skimming down hills without an engine.

By now Chris himself was in college, though his passion for becoming airborne led him into a kind of secondary life as a pilot in the new sport of hang gliding.

FROM THEN ON, THANKS TO CHRIS' ENTHUSIASM AND RISING excitement from Bobby, half our family was lured into the sport. Out of our sons' zeal came a family business, numerous championship wins, a 20th Century Fox movie, and frequent high mountain drama, all detailed in my memoir, *Higher Than Eagles*.

But ultimately our family paid a terrible price. We lost two sons to the sport—first Eric, still an amateur, in 1974, and later, in 1977, Bobby himself. Our oldest son, blown down by a filming helicopter, died as the champion

106

of three countries. With that, letters came from all over the world. From Italy: "If Bobby Wills can get killed, the sport isn't safe for anyone."

We could only react with surprise and deep sadness when we were called "The Kennedys of Hang Gliding."

ALMOST AT THE SAME PERIOD, OUR FOURTH SON, KENNY, WAS spending hours in the high school swimming pool, working out for the Foothill Knights swim team. He swam before and after school for what seemed like thousands of miles. His specialty was the butterfly, probably the most grueling of all the competitive strokes. When he alighted briefly at home, his time was consumed mainly with eating. "What's for dinner, Mom?" he asked—but dinner was never enough. With that much exercise, his body cried out for extra calories—meaning in those days he was seldom far from the refrigerator.

Though Kenny soon swam for UCLA, for years he held the pool butterfly record at UCLA's rival school, USC. As part of his career he eventually tried out for the Olympics ... but his competitors in the prelims proved to be several swimmers who ultimately won Olympic medals.

"What a bummer," Rob said to him later, "if you'd tried out in any other country, you would have made the Olympics."

"I guess I should have swum for Canada," Ken said.

MEANWHILE TRACY, AND THEN OUR YOUNGEST, KIRK, BEGAN TO excel in tennis. For awhile Rob and I had to drive them to tournaments, which, as they improved, seemed to arrive with ever-greater frequency.

When he was only twelve, Kirk earned a California ranking of number twelve in his age group. But what made me proudest was that I never saw him cheat. While often his young opponents, driven by overzealous parents, would call good balls "out," Kirk's flaw tended to land in the other direction. At times uncertainty made him give the other boy the point for a ball that, to us, had clearly landed outside the lines.

In time Tracy, not to be outdone by her brothers, was driving herself to tournaments, always with a competitive attitude ... which I soon realized was even greater than I'd imagined. At one tournament she was playing a ranked player, with no chance to win. From the sidelines, disappointed but not surprised, I watched her lose the first set.

As the girls were changing ends, Tracy hovered over my chair and asked, "What will you give me if I beat her?"

I looked at her through realistic eyes. With this proven opponent, and already down a set, she had absolutely no chance to win. So I said with reckless abandon, "I'll give you a hundred dollars." In those days a hundred dollars was like four hundred today. But I knew my money was safe.

With that, Tracy began turning the match around. Slowly, with an ever-increasing uptick in her skills, she barely nailed the second set.

I was astonished. But not as much as the other girl. Still, there was no chance Tracy could keep up this pace.

Yet somehow she did. By now in perfect stride, Tracy played still better, ever more aggressively, and to the astonishment of all three of us—but especially of her opponent, who began making unforced errors, Tracy easily won the third and defining set.

I was both elated and amazed. And in a way, horrified that I'd been so reckless.

"How did you do that?" I asked. "She's ranked and you're not."

Tracy grinned. "I was playing for a hundred dollars and she wasn't." She held out her hand. "Come on, Mom, you owe me."

"I'll have to go to the bank," I said. "I still can't believe you did this."

"Well, I can. Maybe I should always make bets before I play."

In later years, when she played tennis in college, bets weren't necessary. Trophies were enough—as Tracy and her partner, Jill, proved when they won the small-college national championships in Charleston, South Carolina—just as they'd won the CIF championship in Ojai when they were in high school.

Immediately after Tracy graduated from Cal Poly Pomona, with a degree in kinesiology, the college chose her to be their new tennis coach. Suddenly Tracy was in charge of young women who had, only months earlier, been her teammates.

She described how difficult this became. "The girls wanted to take advantage of the situation," she said. "Once, before an out-of-town tournament, they planned to stay up late, drinking."

She grinned. "I told them, 'if you're up past eleven I'm going to roust you out of your rooms to go run the track before you play.' They decided to give up the liquor and just go to bed." Another smile. "At first it wasn't easy being their boss. But we soon got into the proper rhythm."

In 1983, Tracy and her good friend, Lea, a nationally-ranked player, competed at Wimbledon … followed later by significant women's doubles wins in Orange County.

As it turned out, in later life and through two horrifying marital tragedies, Tracy continued in her sport, and in her fifties, with Susan Wright, she earned a U.S. ranking of number one doubles champion in the fifty-and-over category.

But even tennis would not claim Tracy indefinitely. A few years later, she became a national competitor in the new, still relatively unknown sport of pickleball.

OUR CHILDREN WEREN'T THE ONLY ONES WHOSE LIVES WERE changed by the nearby Red Hill tennis club—as it was once called. For some forty-five years, until our mid-seventies, Rob and I played energetically and often—in my case, about three times a week. Though we each won a few small tournaments and lots of matches, I, for one, could never summon Tracy's cool, no-wavering approach when a match became tight.

Cool under pressure helps explain why Tracy has always been a champion. Which goes as well for her life outside of sports.

CHAPTER EIGHTEEN

Tragedy Brings a Reunion

WHEN MY FATHER, TED, BECAME A SORT OF LONG-DISTANCE WRITING mentor, I began to feel, once more, a new connection, and the budding of a relationship I'd been missing most of my childhood. For a few years, manuscripts and advice flowed back and forth across the country.

With that first sale of a story on hang gliding, it seemed my career was launched. With surprising ease, I sold additional stories, but always on the same subject.

And then, with the hang gliding deaths of our two sons, our world came crashing down.

IT WAS ONLY AFTER CHRIS INVESTIGATED THAT ROB AND I LEARNED how and why Bobby died, that the accident had in no way been his fault. Instead, his death resulted from the deliberate malfeasance of a filming helicopter ... with the same pilot who'd filmed our kids for a hang gliding movie in Greece. Bobby had once said, "I'll never fly again with a helicopter; it's too dangerous." But he trusted George, and George was at the controls.

Now, while ferrying the photographer who was filming Bobby as they made an ad for Willys Jeep, the helicopter pilot was persuaded to steal extra footage and guide the copter into a forbidden area. All too well George was aware of the danger, that a helicopter left behind a deadly wake.

Sadly, Bobby was on the backside of a turn and never knew the helicopter had been there. As he completed his turn, he encountered the wild downdraft which blew him to the ground.

For both funerals, the second arranged by Chris, my father flew cross-country to be with our family and comfort us. How well I remember his warmth when he arrived—comforting but not effusive.

Thanks to the movies Chris showed at the funeral, Rob and I were given a modicum of relief. Here was Bobby, high above the earth in his butterfly hang glider, looking utterly content and in his element. It seemed he was once more doing what he was born to do.

Two days later, before he left, Ted suggested that Rob and I might want to play tennis. Immediately I was overwhelmed by guilt.

How can I go back to my favorite sport when my son has just died? I thought. Reluctantly, we played. But for the first hour, with a sense of despair, of heaviness.

With that, I learned a few truisms about grief. After a death in the family, you will always feel chagrined the first time you enjoy yourself—or the first time you laugh.

Chapter Nineteen

Nerds to the Rescue

My first book sale was almost an accident. Within a year of Bobby's death I left our hang gliding manufacturing company, Wills Wings, to return home and write books. I couldn't stay on, trying to keep alive a company that had been the indirect cause of so much grief.

Only one topic occurred to me—a memoir about the craziness, then sadness, of a mother running a hang gliding company. In spite of our losses, the early years contained both humor and drama.

One of my best friends, Patty Teal, an author's agent, began sending out my completed manuscript ... but predictably, she received nothing but rejections.

Yet Saul Cohen from Prentice-Hall—an editor with his own imprint— mentioned in his rejection letter, "They sent me the manuscript because they know I'm doing a series on unpowered flight."

With that Patty Teal, traditionally an opportunist of the best kind, suggested, "Why don't you offer to do a different book for him?"

"I can't do that, Patty," I said. "I'm too involved in my own book."

"Well, at least ask," she said, "What can it hurt?"

Expecting nothing, I sent Saul Cohen a telegram. "At my agent's prodding, I offer myself as an expert to write a fiction or non-fiction book on hang gliding. Qualifications include ... " and I listed a dozen reasons that backed up my bold claim.

Three days later, Cohen called. "I think it's an interesting idea for a woman to write a book on hang gliding. Why don't you send me a proposal?"

"Oh, sure, Mr. Cohen, I'll be glad to do that."

The minute we hung up, I called Patty. "What's a proposal?"

"Well," she said, laughing, "it's a selling tool. A way to convince an editor you can actually write a book." But that was all she suggested, leaving a noticeable gap on specifics.

With nothing much to go on, I did what I could: I bluffed. Even as I hurriedly typed whatever occurred to me, I knew I was faking. After composing a possible first chapter, I wrote lists of all the areas in which I had expertise. After awhile, my so-called proposal became believable, even to me. *Maybe, after all, I AM an expert.*

My submission obviously convinced editor Saul Cohen. During a second phone call he offered to send a contract. "And Prentice-Hall is proposing an advance of ten-thousand dollars. Will that be all right?"

Ten thousand dollars? "Oh yes," I said, almost choking on a sudden surge of amazement. "That will be fine, Mr. Cohen." Though I tried to convey nonchalance, *this is no big deal,* I could hear my voice shaking. He must have guessed I was covering up ... about like a scantily-clad actor caught on the wrong side of the curtain. The truth is, I was so excited I could hardly breathe.

Once the call ended, I went flying across the house to share the news with Rob.

"You really ARE an expert," he said. "And for once, Babe, you're getting paid for it."

Eight months and numerous scary and uncertain moments later (and with considerable help from both Chris and Betty-Jo), I mailed in the manuscript. Within a month Saul Cohen sent me the first galleys of my new book, which he titled: *MANBIRDS: Hang Gliders and Hang Gliding.*

When the volume was later listed by Library Journal as one of the year's 100-Best Books on Science and Technology, my reaction was typical; once more I imagined I was through forever with rejection slips.

The truth came later. My publication with Prentice-Hall was simply another down-payment on a fraught-with-rejection writing career.

WHEN MY CAREER ACTUALLY BEGAN, ALL WRITERS USED TYPEWRITERS … which meant typing a final draft was agony. Every mistake—and usually they were plentiful—involved going back and whiting out the error, then making the correction on one to three carbons. If the goof-up was serious, you had to re-type the entire page.

Re-typing was required even in drafts. For me, and possibly others, until sentences were cleanly typed I couldn't really gauge their impact. Composing an entire book was a task comprised largely of re-typing.

Earlier than most authors, I began writing on a computer … and all because my brother, Allan, a computer whiz with NASA, persuaded me I was using an antiquated tool. In the early 1980s, he talked me into buying four components: the all-important "DOS" unit, a screen, a keyboard, and a printer. Because he lived an hour's drive away, he'd be down later, he said, to assemble the parts.

I remember arriving home and calling to our youngest son, "Come over here, Kirk, and help me carry this computer upstairs to my office."

For a moment he stared down into my trunk, filled with cardboard boxes. Before he lifted a finger he asked in a tone of wonder, "How many of 'em did you buy?"

I burst out laughing because I'd been astonished, too. "Only one," I said. "But it has lots of sections."

Still baffled, he shook his head.

MY SECOND SURPRISE CAME LATER WHEN ALLAN ARRIVED TO GET me started. In his hands he carried two enormous loose-leaf notebooks. "These are the instructions," he said. "They'll tell you how everything works."

I gasped. "I have to read ALL THAT?"

"Well, I guess. But I can tell you most of it."

And luckily he could, because my initial glance into the first notebook did not bode well. I began reading sentences full of words that for me had no meaning … words and expressions I'd never seen or heard of. Within a few pages it became obvious that the notebooks were written for people like Allan who worked at NASA. For as far as I scanned, I never found a single sentence that conveyed meaning.

"These are impossible, Allan," I said, thumping the notebook as he assembled the computer. "I can read English just fine. But with these pages, I'll never be able to figure out anything."

"Yeah, that's probably true," he admitted. "Running a computer is actually a lot easier than those instructions imply. They assume you know a lot more than you do." He grinned. "Don't worry, Maralys, I'll help you."

I closed the fat notebook, plopped it on top of the other, and never referred to either again. From that day forward, Allan became my tutor. Which made me realize why only I, among my writing friends, was working on such an advanced gadget. In the beginning, they weren't created for ordinary, non-technical people like me. Those were the days, in the early 80s, when computers were designed strictly for nerds.

Together, Allan and I created ten pages of simple instructions: *When this happens, press this button.* Those pages became my bible. One day I said to Allan, "Only YOU understand what I don't know. Why don't we work together and write a book … we'd call it, *Computers for Idiots.*

He never gave it more than a moment's thought. "Nah … I don't have time."

"But lots of people would buy it," I said. "We really should do it." He shook his head, dismissing the whole idea.

My brother was smart, but for once not smart enough.

If only I'd managed to persuade him. Within a year, Allan and I would have been rich. Really, really rich.

WHEN, AFTER SEVERAL ENTIRE REVISIONS, MY MEMOIR ABOUT BOBBY received nothing but rejections, Patty Teal persuaded me to try writing a romance. "Your own book hasn't sold," she said, "and romances are doing well, selling like hotcakes."

"But Patty, I've never read one," I said. "How can I possibly write one?"

"Well, read a few, see what you think."

So I bought six romances and read them all. One was pretty good, and another passable. The other four were terrible. *I can do better than those*, I thought. *Maybe I should try*.

But I knew I had deficiencies: with a skimpy imagination, I'd be hard put to come up with a plot. So I approached my daughter-in-law, the most omnivorous reader I knew … whose degree was in library science. "Betty-Jo, you read all the time. How would you like to help me write a romance?"

"A romance?" she asked, surprised. "But that's not what I read."

"Me neither. But I'll give you the books I just finished. You can see what you think."

A week later she said, "I see what you mean, Maralys. We can certainly do better than most of these."

Together we decided she'd come up with the plot and I'd do the writing. As it turned out, we each did some of both.

And thus, for the next few years, Betty-Jo and I wrote and sold four romances, one every other year. Ultimately we were published by both Harlequin and Silhouette, and on each momentous occasion our two husbands helped us celebrate with a dinner out.

When we finally gave up on writing romances, each of us had a different reason. Betty-Jo was now ultra-busy, pregnant with her fourth child, and I, who'd been persuaded we needed to choose plots exploring parts of our own lives, decided I was running out of personal experiences.

From then on, with never a thought of giving up writing altogether, I began looking for new topics to write about—while still ardently seeking a publisher for *Higher Than Eagles*, the book-of-my-heart.

And then one day Betty-Jo, now in her ninth month of pregnancy, got on the phone after I'd spoken to her oldest, seven-year-old Christy. I'd been presented with a proposal so far-fetched Betty-Jo and I both thought it laughable.

Even now, I can scarcely believe how her daughter's crazy idea all worked out.

CHAPTER TWENTY

The Sleepless Sleepover

ABOUT MID-OCTOBER OF 1984, JUST AS I DECIDED THIS MIGHT BE our first year without a single reportable vignette, our seven-year-old granddaughter, Christy, called me up. I remember I was riding my stationery bike at the time, and that the pedals stopped turning abruptly.

She asked in her sweet, small voice, "You won't mind, will you, Grandma Maralys, if I have my birthday party at your house?"

"What kind of party?" I asked.

"A slumber party," she said in that same sweet voice-of-impossible wishes.

"Mind?" I echoed, astonished. "Christy, this is the first time I've even heard of it!" Then there was my second reaction, a tolerant, almost smug attitude—how could I mind what I had no intention of doing? "What's the matter with *your* house, Christy?"

"My Mom doesn't want to have it."

Well, I thought, *that's what's the matter with my house, too.* Memories of old slumber parties came back: the few Tracy had had fifteen years earlier were all party and no slumbering. Furthermore, these days I was having some trouble slumbering myself. I could just imagine trying to patrol a gaggle of giggling seven-year-olds all night, followed by a week of trying to recover.

I said, "Let me talk to your mother, Honey."

Betty-Jo came on, laughing.

I said, "She's kidding, isn't she?"

"No she's serious. I told her you wouldn't want to do it, I was sure you wouldn't, but she insisted on asking." Betty-Jo laughed again. "*I'm* not going to host that party. I certainly can't imagine your wanting to."

"It's a pretty crazy idea, all right. But I give her a "G" for gumption.

Which is all I remember of how that unthinkable night came about. There must have been some transition, some kind of psychological shaping that occurred between Christy's crazy proposal and her two grandparents agreeing—arguments, pleading, or the lot, but they've all slipped my mind. The only thing that stands out is Rob's astonishing attitude—that he was absolutely gallant!

I do recall saying, "But no more than five altogether, Christy," and Betty-Jo calling up some time later and explaining apologetically, "I hate to tell you this, Maralys, but Christy has social obligations ..." meaning five was out of the question, it was eight girls or none. And of that eight four were two sets of twins, one in each pair named Kelly—which, with Christy's younger sister would mean three Kellys altogether and four with faces you couldn't tell apart.

Betty-Jo tried to prepare me. "The invitations say six o'clock, Maralys, and the girls will show up at my house at exactly six and not one will be even five minutes late." Then she amended it. "Actually, some of them will appear at five to six."

Over the next week Betty-Jo reminded me several times about the odd and literal tendencies of little girls who come to parties at the stated hour. Anxiously, "You won't be late, will you, Maralys?" Betty-Jo was then almost nine months pregnant and reluctant to deal with eight extra girls, if only for a few minutes.

I'm happy to say I got there right at six. However, it wasn't soon enough, because Betty-Jo's house was already filled with six mothers, eight girls clutching cabbage patch dolls (I'd thought those ugly little dolls were in short supply—apparently not short enough), and a mountain of sleeping bags and suitcases, enough stuff for a month on safari. I stared at the pile of equipment. All this for one night? Were the mothers thinking, perhaps, I was going to keep them indefinitely?

My eye traveled along the line of little heads. All those eyes looked back at me suspiciously (some of them identical eyes in identical heads), and I thought, *Oh, boy …*

Mothers helped me load up—pile after pile into Betty-Jo's big van, and then the girls arranged themselves dutifully, all strapped in and feet suspended off the floor, and Chris came out and gave them a little lecture about keeping the noise level down and how if I raised my right hand, all were to stop talking instantly. I didn't admit to Chris that there was no possibility of raising my right hand while driving his large and unfamiliar van, that I'd be lucky just to get everyone to my house without denting his equipment. I didn't believe in scaring him, so I let him give his lecture and I drove off with what sounded like a thousand birds behind me, all chirping at once.

Our first stop was McDonald's, and there I witnessed what must be a Friday night phenomenon all over America. The place was packed. Absolutely loaded to the gunnels with families, of which there seemed to be ten hyperkinetic children to every responsible adult. The noise in there was incredible. It would have been worse without the slides and merry-go-round outside. As it was, kids raced through the lines and between our legs and down the aisles, while the grownups stood in line eyes-front-and-center and pretended they didn't notice.

Rob met us there, and I could see my own reaction in his expression. A quick onceover and he asked, "What is this, a zoo?" He kept standing there, staring. Later he said it was like being in a foreign country, that there wasn't anybody in the place like us.

Resourceful Christy found us a booth large enough to more or less accommodate our mob, and there the kids devoured Chicken-McNuggets, and stared without shame at two Tustin High cheerleaders. Our little girls were frankly overcome by the flashy outfits. "Oooh, they're so PRETTY!" "Should we tell them they're pretty?" and so on. Finally Christy led a raid on the older girls, a brave foray in which eight little girls dashed down the aisle to the two amazed teenagers, delivered their worshipful messages and scampered back. Soon the older girls left with the proud look of goddesses.

I gave Rob the job of driving the van with its load of chirping birds back to our house, a dubious assignment when the birds turned into mockingbirds and imitated everything he said. When he coughed, eight girls coughed, and when he said "What's all this?" back came a chorus of "What's all this?" and being young they had the energy to keep it up the whole way, giggling and thinking they were being terribly funny. Rob thought they were something less than hilarious. "It could have gotten tiresome," he said, "if we'd had to go more than three miles."

Back home, the girls buried one end of our family room under sleeping bags, played the organized games Christy wanted, devoured the ice-cream-sundaes-with-choice-of-topping she wanted, (I kept the portions small, not wanting anyone to get sick), and then danced in the living room to Rob's records. Such dancing! Hips swaying. Hands gesturing. Heads tilting. More like ages seventeen than seven. Rob kept playing records because they were so entertaining to watch.

Bedtime, and eight nighties went on, and then someone said, "I take tumbling!" and she cart wheeled across the family room in her nightie and panties—and then so did seven others. Except the last girl gave us rather a surprise. Hands down, she began her cartwheel, and up went the legs, and down went her nightie, and to everyone's astonishment, she was just like the others—except without the panties. I thought her legs would never come down. I also thought it was time we did something else. Like go to bed.

All in one room, the eight filled the family room literally wall to wall. In only one minute girls were complaining about feet in their faces, so we split them into two rooms.

An hour later nobody was sleeping. But somebody was out in the family room complaining that she "felt sick." And I asked, "Like you have to throw up?" and she shook her head Yes, and I held that one on my lap until her mother came. I was waiting to see who would be next.

Eventually our little girls began sleeping and Rob and I went to bed. I figured they'd give us eight hours if we were very lucky.

They didn't and we weren't. Before seven Christy was in our room proclaiming, "Kelly's vomiting!"

An announcement like that wakes you right up. Rob groaned, "It had to happen," and I leaped to my feet, and sure enough one of the Kellys was on her knees next to the potty.

Kneeling in the bathroom was all she ever did, but alarmed out of further sleep, I whipped out a nice breakfast of scrambled eggs, only to discover Christy had fed everyone doughnuts and now they were all too full for real food.

Well, Betty-Jo had warned me. She'd said, "Just give them doughnuts for breakfast, that's all they'll eat anyway," and I thought, *No child leaves my house with a doughnut breakfast.*

But they all did. Among the seven survivors, no more than two bites of eggs were consumed, but Rob and I were left with more scrambled eggs than we could possibly eat. Which proves people like us should leave the raising of kids to people like Betty-Jo ... the professionals!

Back when Chris and Betty-Jo were married, we began a family tradition—that we would tag along on all our kids' honeymoons. Since Rob and I gave them a four-day head start and ultimately paid the bill, our children were happy with the arrangement.

That first honeymoon trip brought us world-recognized hang gliding adventures that have been amply covered in *Higher Than Eagles*, the memoir that was published fourteen years after its first draft. Thanks to great enthusiasm from Longstreet Press, the memoir ultimately received five movie options, including from Disney and the producers of *Northern Exposure*.

Our next honeymoon trip was also to Hawaii—with our daughter, Tracy, when she married Geoff Worley. We all adored him. But the repercussions from that trip were different in every way from those we relished with Chris and Betty-Jo.

Sadly, most of the fallout was anything but good.

CHAPTER TWENTY-ONE

We Lost a Prince

TRACY'S HONEYMOON WITH GEOFF WORLEY STARTED OUT WELL enough. We all loved Geoff, whom Tracy had met as her partner in a college basketball refereeing class. "Just watch what I do," Geoff explained … an expert who dashed around the court, guiding her with tact and obvious expertise.

Geoff was six-four, a Tom Seleck look-alike, and extraordinarily good-natured.

For this second honeymoon the family chose the island of Maui, where Rob found a hotel perched on the top of a cliff. Up there the ocean wind was so vigorous that our draperies took flight and attempted to soar off and circle the living room. Only the strongest drapery rings kept them anchored anywhere near the window.

Most of our family came along. There, for the first time Chris (already an orthopedic surgeon), happened to view Geoff's knee. Until then Geoff— both a basketball and volleyball star at Cal Poly Pomona—had kept it covered with a knee brace.

What Chris saw was a large, irregular, and multi-shaded mole. He shook his head. "Geoff, when you get home you'd better have that mole checked out. I don't like the way it looks."

"Okay."

"How long have you had it?"

"As long as I can remember, all my life."

"But now it's pretty big." Chris paused. "And nobody's ever said anything?"

"He doesn't go to doctors much," said Tracy. "His mom and dad are strong Christian Scientists."

"But I'm less into it than they are," said Geoff.

"He'll go to a doctor when he needs to," Tracy added.

"I wouldn't wait," said Chris. "I'd make that appointment first thing."

Geoff nodded. "Okay. Gotcha, Chris."

THAT WAS ONLY THE VACATION'S FIRST MEDICAL ISSUE. TOWARD THE end of the trip, Rob and I were playing a vigorous game of tennis. I rarely beat him in singles, but I never accepted a loser's attitude. With him, I played all out.

Halfway into the match, I tossed the ball up to serve. When I jerked my left arm downward, I felt something snap. The pain was immediate. "Oh, oh," I said, and dropped my racquet. "Something's wrong with my left arm."

Rob ran around to my side. "Let's see the arm."

"Nothing to see," I said. "But I can't lift it. Look—it won't raise even to my waist." I tried … but to no avail. The arm had suddenly become useless.

"Guess we're through playing," Rob said. "Wonder what's the problem."

Chris knew immediately. "You've torn your rotator cuff, Mom."

"So now what?"

"Well, give it a rest. It might heal on its own."

But it didn't. At least not for the rest of the trip. For the remainder of our stay, I was one-armed and half an invalid. An arm that can't be raised above your waist isn't good for much.

The arm was no better after we returned home. While Chris kept promising nature would come to my rescue, his partner in the office didn't think so.

Thus, within a week I underwent rotator cuff surgery. After a couple of months of therapy I could once more raise my arm above my head … but largely because I was both faithful and vigorous about doing my rehab exercises.

I am not a stubborn German for nothing.

WITHIN OUR FIRST WEEK HOME, GEOFF WENT TO OUR FAMILY dermatologist. I happened to be outside his house when he got out of the car. The bandage on his knee was huge.

"Wow!" I said. "They must have done a major job on you."

He nodded. "The doctor went pretty deep. Much deeper than I imagined. It took quite a while."

"Does it hurt?"

He passed it off. "Not as bad as you'd think."

Soon Tracy and Geoff received the pathology report. When she told us the news, Tracy was white and shaken. "It's melanoma—class three, deep. He'll need more surgery, the doctor said. And they'll have to remove some lymph nodes."

The second time, the surgeon excavated a cavern under Geoff's knee. And he also removed the nearest lymph nodes, all from his left side.

To Tracy's relief, the follow-up pathology report was encouraging. "The surgical margins are clear. And so are his lymph nodes," she said. "Thank God."

"Oh, Tracy. Then we can stop worrying."

"I guess so, Mom. He's lucky. The doctor was really relieved."

EIGHT YEARS WENT BY WITH GEOFF IN GOOD HEALTH. HE AND Tracy had two children—first a daughter, Jamie, and three years later a son, Dane. I can still see Geoff mowing their front lawn trailed by an eager little boy, and how often the very tall father slowed to allow his son to catch up.

How regularly Rob and I went to their home for dinner, and how invariably Geoff greeted us with a generous smile and a big, "Hi, there!" as though we were *his* parents as well as Tracy's. For both Rob and me, Geoff became another son … the one who, from the start, welcomed us into his heart.

Even now, as I look back on all the hours we spent with Geoff, Tracy, and their children, I feel a lump in my throat, and the start of tears I'm helpless to control.

IN THE EIGHTH YEAR OF THEIR MARRIAGE, WHILE GEOFF WAS coaching his five year-old daughter's soccer team, he became aware of a pain in his left side that made running difficult. He needed to dash along the sidelines of the field—but suddenly couldn't.

He explained to Tracy, "I think I've pulled a muscle."

When the pain grew worse, he went to see Chris. After an x-ray, Chris said, "You have a mass there, Geoff. We'll have to check it out."

"I think it's an abscess, Mom," Chris reported when I called his office later. "We're doing a needle biopsy."

The next day we spoke again. I sensed Chris was choked up, maybe crying. "It's not an abscess, Mom. It's a return of the melanoma."

"Oh God," I said. "Oh, God. That's awful."

"It's worse than awful," he said, and went silent.

"Where can Dad and I see him?"

"He's in the hospital. Better go right away."

When Rob and I arrived at St. Joseph's, Tracy and her kids were already seated, her children in her lap. A deep, sad silence hung over the room. Nobody knew what to say.

While we were there, an oncologist stopped by. The man sat by Geoff's bed, reading from technical papers.

I sensed that Geoff was only half listening. Instead, he peeked out from behind the man's papers and waved at his children.

Sadness yanked at my soul, pulled at my body. I couldn't stand the sensation. "Let's go to the cafeteria," I said to Rob. "For a snack."

We were only there a short time when I said, "I need to go home." But at home the inner pain continued. "I have to get back to the hospital," I said.

Only later did I realize the anguish of Geoff's illness was so intense, I was trying to run away—to escape from my own hurting skin.

For the next three months Tracy's neighbors brought casseroles, almost nonstop. Midway, with Betty-Jo keeping the kids, Rob and I took the two adults to Hawaii. But by then Geoff was in a wheelchair, largely unable to walk. The trip was anything but a success. Geoff tried to smile, to comfort us … but we three were in agony over his obvious disability. We soon went home.

Months of hopeless treatment in several hospitals followed the trip. The melanoma crept into Geoff's brain. On one occasion when I took him for brain radiation, he couldn't stop talking about the small children who'd been with him in the waiting room. "It's so unfair," he said. "Some of them are so young."

Geoff never uttered a word about himself.

For two weeks, because he was now being treated at a nearby cancer center, Tracy left him with his parents in San Diego while she returned home to be with the children. Geoff's father, less deeply into religion, took him for his treatments.

Still steeped in Christian Science, Geoff's mother refused to go near a hospital.

When Tracy returned for a visit, Geoff said, "Leave some morphine tablets under my pillow, Trace. Mom won't give them to me."

Tracy was horrified. "Come home," she said. "You'll have to come back with me." On a rainy afternoon, Tracy drove several long, dangerous hours up the freeway. Trucks roared by, pelting them with water. Besides Geoff, she had two children in the car. Once she had to stop and stuff a napkin between his teeth because her patient was having a seizure.

That drive home with Geoff and the kids was one of Tracy's worst moments.

By mid-February, Geoff was near death. In his last hour, while his parents went out to dinner, Tracy turned up the house music and crawled into the hospital bed with him. As she did, tears rolled down Geoff's face.

When I arrived, a few minutes later, the music was still blasting. But Geoff was gone.

I was stunned and shocked. Devastated for Tracy, but also for myself.

For me, the loss of Geoff was more excruciating, if anything, than the loss of my own two sons. Geoff had consistently savored our friendship, our love, with never a negative word. But more. In subtle ways he let us know the love was mutual. Rob and I knew we'd never know another man like him.

In this nonstop tale of sadness, one devastating moment remains stark. How well I remember the scene. The funeral was over, and Tracy and her kids and I were in the family room, with Dane sitting on the couch. For no special reason, Dane, only two, began crying out, "I want my Daddy! I want my Daddy!"

His tone, the desperation in his voice, clutched at me, brought a stinging to my throat, made all of us feel terrible.

Five-year-old Jamie was able to endure just so much. After a few seconds, she leaned over the couch and said sternly, "Dane, stop crying! He's never coming back!"

As she jolted all of us into silence, I stared at her, this very young girl who already understood what none of us could say aloud, who took charge when we adults felt helpless. This was the moment when Jamie became one of the pillars in Dane's life.

For the next ten years, all of us, every family member in Tracy's vicinity, found our lives profoundly changed.

CHAPTER TWENTY-TWO

The Aftermath

LUCKY FOR HER, TRACY LIVED IN A NEIGHBORHOOD WHERE KINDNESS prevailed. During Geoff's illness and afterward, they formed prayer circles. Neighbors brought food, gifts for the children, continuous offers of handyman repairs. This went on longer than anyone could have predicted. For months, Tracy was steeped in affection, in helpfulness, in whatever friends could do to ease a widow's pain.

ROB AND I DID WHAT WE COULD. FOR THE TWO OF US IT MEANT intensified roles as grandparents. Tracy and her children now needed us more than ever. *Somebody*, besides Tracy, had to be there for baby-sitting, for the kids' sports events, for advice and just plain listening. Sometimes it seemed we spent nearly as much time in Tracy's home as our own.

Geoff's death caught me in the middle of trying to finish the second book of a three-book contract with Presidio Press. Though I managed to turn in a long partial for an oil drama set in Nigeria, plus an equally-long summary (thanks to a number of interviews with experts), the editor didn't like what I'd done ... and by then I didn't have the psychic energy to start over.

My writing career came to an overlong halt. I was still teaching novel-writing, but now more of my free hours went to grand-mothering. And the same went for Rob. Sometimes it felt like we'd been given a special privilege—an up close relationship with Jamie and Dane.

One of my first observations concerned the interplay between the kids themselves. For reasons I never fully understood, the two didn't fight.

My own kids (mostly thanks to our oldest, Bobby), fought all the time, which, for me, became the nadir of motherhood. Nothing was more irritating—make that upsetting—than the howls of a child being picked on by his brother. Never much of a disciplinarian, I was unable to figure out how to make all that kid-to-kid conflict go away. I reasoned, I shouted, I scolded, I remonstrated, but nothing seemed to work. Too often, Rob got home from late from work, and seldom saw the worst of it—the kid-to-kid dramas which, around dinnertime, rose to unacceptable levels of shouting and yes, shrieking. "Stop it!" I'd shout, and ran to close the windows so the neighbors wouldn't hear the racket.

For our family, it took a period of "sending away" of that oldest boy to his grandparents before peace settled over our household.

None of that was an issue with Tracy's kids. Neither child had a temper, and likewise, neither was given to deliberately provoking the other. If anything, Jamie was mostly a protector and guide for her younger brother.

I could see that Dane listened to Jamie, enjoyed her attention, and soon considered her something of a mentor.

As for us, during the ten years Tracy was alone (she was only 35 when Geoff died), Rob and I partially lived our lives, but to a lesser degree we also participated in our daughter's three-person family.

I remember the hours that Rob spent sitting in his family-room chair and tossing balls at the two kids (which he'd done earlier for our own children).

He'd shout, "CATCH!" and then, after a faked throw of a small ball in a certain direction, he'd take a different aim and send one child or another dashing after it. The game usually went on for the better part of an hour. In the process, I could see the kids' growing perceptions about the ultimate direction of the missile. I noticed they were increasingly able to figure out its course and dash to the right spot … then ever quicker to catch it midair and toss it back.

In later years, when Jamie and Dane began playing tennis, volleyball, and badminton, I suspect their athleticism was aided by Rob's early frolics in the family room.

For Tracy, in the years after Geoff, her children, then sports, were her biggest consolation.

After perhaps a year of widowhood, she was appointed as a member of Tustin's Parks and Recreation Commission. She'd only held the position a year when a friend urged her to run for Tustin's City Council. With Rob and me and others babysitting, Tracy ran and won.

For twelve years she remained on the Council and, for four of those years, she served as the city's mayor.

When President Clinton came to town as he ran for a second term, Tracy was one of the supporting speakers.

I was lucky enough to be there when Cal Poly invited her back to be honored as that year's Distinguished Alumna. In a speech I will forever remember, she described in touching terms what her life had become after losing her husband, and how she coped as a council member of Tustin—and then its mayor.

Yet she spoke passionately about what she considered to be her most important job among the three—her role as a mother. With that, she quoted Jackie Kennedy. "If you fail at the job of raising your children, nothing else much matters."

For the next ten years, Tracy dated a variety of men, but none came close to replacing Geoff. Often it took a few months before the fatal defect (or defects) showed up.

The dating game included some strange moments. One suitor epitomized the problem: though Tracy knew the handsome tennis player with whom she was having coffee was divorced with two young children, she only found out surreptitiously that Romeo had left behind TWO families ... and that the never-mentioned additional family came with three additional kids.

And then one day, as mayor of Tustin, Tracy was asked to appear in an ad about the city.

The man who videotaped her for the footage was Brad Hagen. In his use of video equipment, Brad was unusually creative, and soon he and Tracy were dating. Though Brad had never been married, he did not exhibit any of the traits Tracy found so objectionable in others.

At the end of two years, when Jamie was fifteen, and Dane twelve, Brad and Tracy were married in the Tustin Presbyterian Church. In spite of his initial strictness with her children, "Hey, get those shoes off the stairs!" he railed, the kids welcomed Brad into their home.

"I can see him changing," I said to Rob after a while, happy to observe that gradually Brad became more relaxed and accepting of his role as a parent.

Finally Tracy had a father figure to accompany her to the children's sports events.

By then, sports had become important in the lives of both Jamie and Dane. Jamie graduated from middle school as "Athlete of the Year," and three years later, Dane finished there as the MVP in tennis, basketball, and volleyball.

Since high school required that athletes make a choice, both chose volleyball at Foothill High.

At age 18, Jamie enrolled in Cal Poly, San Luis Obispo, intent on earning a degree in landscape architecture.

By then Dane was increasingly visible as a major player in Foothill High's volleyball team. Tracy, Rob, and I (and often Chris and Betty-Jo), went to his local games. And here I offer a grandmotherly note—that it never ceased to amaze me that Dane was willing, post game, to offer me a hug—in full view of his teammates.

With off-season membership in a club team, The Riptides, Dane's volleyball skills were constantly honed.

And here I'm driven to relate a story about Dane's final participation, as a high school senior, in a national volleyball tournament.

When I included this long story in our annual Christmas newsletter—which Rob refuses to call anything except Our Annual Report—family members dubbed that year's offering as *The Dane-ual Report*. So perhaps an apology is due the family—that here it is. Again.

Until i got mixed up with my grandson, Dane, I supposed that most male athleticism, of the super tall variety, involved basketball. Then, with Dane, I entered a new world of giants—the volleyball players. Since these athletes appear only rarely on television, the best place to view them is a tournament ... where you find yourself dwarfed by streams of six-foot-eight guys striding across the arena in great gulps, accompanied by bean-pole friends and trailed by six-foot-four fathers. You begin wondering—Where do they find the eight foot mattresses? The size 15 shoes?

Dane has never been one of them. Though his father, Geoff, was six-four, as a high school junior Dane seemed to hover around six feet. Finally, by the end of his senior year, he squeaked out a meager six-two.

During the three years in which college coaches with clipboards study club volleyball teams and jot down certain names, Dane's teams always did well in the yearly blowout, the National Junior Olympics. A silver medal one year, a bronze another. Various college coaches watched him, in particular the assistant coach from the University of Southern California. But none of the coaches from UCLA (his preferred school), even glanced his way, and we all knew why: traditionally, UCLA was interested only in men six-five and above.

Still, in the NCAA-designated recruitment weeks before his senior year, SC courted Dane with a vengeance—with all the official campus tours and enthusiastic emails ... and our family, with its eight UCLA degrees, managed to drum up limited enthusiasm for Dane's joining the enemy.

But on one of those family tours, Tracy picked up bad vibes. None of the coaches would look her in the eye. When they got home, she said to Dane, "Why don't you send an e-mail to UCLA? What have you got to lose?"

So Dane sent them a "Hail Mary" letter—a kind of verbal spiral where the whole game is won or lost. After admitting that other schools had courted him, he told the rest of his story—that he'd always wanted to go to UCLA, that his family had all those degrees, that he'd won the state beach volleyball championship three times, that he'd been named all-this, and all-that.

Meanwhile, he'd been trying to re-confirm with SC—and couldn't. No phone calls returned, no emails answered. Finally, a day after he sent his UCLA letter, he managed to reach the head SC coach and was told, "We're cutting our bench. We don't have room for you." Learning later that the enthusiastic assistant coach had been fired didn't help. Clearly, SC had been trying to avoid telling Dane the truth until the recruitment deadline had passed—a kind of, "We don't want you, but we don't want you playing for anyone else," tactic.

For one hour Dane was devastated. He'd turned down several other schools and now, as the dumpee from SC, he had nowhere to go.

An hour later everything changed. On his computer was a return email from UCLA. "We would love to have you play for UCLA. Send us your transcripts immediately." And presto, he was on the UCLA team. With a partial scholarship.

As a family, we considered that the highlight of Dane's volleyball career. The sport had brought him what he'd wanted from the beginning— acceptance to the school of his dreams. How were we to know that was only the beginning?

It seemed an anti-climax that in late June he'd be playing his last Junior Olympics. Though we could not imagine that anything life-changing was riding on the tournament, his sister, Jamie, and I opted to join Tracy and Brad in Atlanta.

By now Dane's Riptides team had acquired a new player, a six-six giant who'd been a top pick by all the colleges. With Murray aboard, the Riptides played a last qualifying tournament in Anaheim. Rob and I went to all the matches, but soon wished we hadn't. Our new giant was a miracle point-getter mid-game, but on crucial points … well, let's just say they seldom went our way. Each time we desperately needed a kill, Murray hit it ten feet wide or deep into the net. Likewise with serves. We lost four matches in a row. I could hardly stand to watch. All of us in the stands wished someone would tell the coach, *When it's tight, take out Murray.*

I began wondering, *What's the point of going to Atlanta?* Thanks to those losses, our heretofore winning team had qualified 9th. What could we hope to accomplish, starting at 9th—when even a third-place finish seemed unlikely.

Well, along with Jamie, I went anyway—and on day two walked into the country's most impressive indoor stadium. Instead of the 20 volleyball courts contained within our sizeable Anaheim Sports Center, this convention center housed around forty. From one end of the room, you couldn't see the courts at the other. And now at eight a.m., on a Thursday, I sat down in one of the folding chairs that lined the court—and watched our team lose. We played Sports Performance from Chicago—one game to them, one to us, and then in the tiebreaker game, first to 15, we lost 15-17. Tracy leaned my way, "You know, Mom, if we lose another match, we're out of the running for gold. The best we can do is … well, 25th!.."

Somehow, miraculously that Thursday, we struggled through two more matches and won them both—the second after a third-game match-point against us. Instead of finishing third in our pool and dropping into the consolation round, we'd managed somehow to end up first.

Two more days to play. On Friday, with Dane suggesting to Murray that he toss his serves higher and farther from his body, Murray served beautifully, and with Dane shouting encouragement to Murray on his kills, and making crucial kills himself, and the others hanging tough, we won our two matches, both in two games. Against all odds, we were now in the round of eight. Out of 92 teams.

Tracy sat with me in those chairs and calculated tomorrow's chances … how with this win, that loss, and that win, we might yet earn a bronze medal. As it was, we could do no worse than fifth place. "Well," she said, "it beats 9th!"

On Saturday, the 4th of July, everything came down to three matches. We won the first rather easily, and I kept thinking, *Hey, that was nice!!* Four teams left. *Okay, then, let's head for the bronze.*

But first we had to face a giant killer, Manhattan Beach Surf, who, all tournament long, had demolished everyone. Never lost a match. Never struggled. As I sat down on a folding chair, I heard a player from another team ask his friend, "Who do you think will win?" and the friend said, "Manhattan Beach in two."

Well, that's what I figured, too. We'd lose this one for sure. But maybe … possibly … eke out a win in the playoff match for third. Not too bad.

And indeed, right from the start, the third-place playoff loomed large. Manhattan Surf took us right down, 10-3 in the first game, headed straight for a winning 25 points. Clearly we were doomed. Then somehow we won a couple of points. Still doomed. Then a couple more points. Well, I'm dying here, because we're a sure loss. Yet somehow we're winning a few more points. And Dane is playing like a champ, getting one kill after another. And Murray is getting the rest. And nobody is shanking balls.

Then, inexplicably, in this first game we catch up. And suddenly take the lead. A small lead, only a point or two, with Manhattan Surf constantly pounding the ball, bringing them up even. Yet we hold on, never more than a point or two ahead. To a man, our boys scramble like doomed gladiators, constantly "digging," saving ourselves from the other team's kills. At 25-all, we're tied. And then we blow past them with two points and win the first game, 27-25. All I can think is, *At least they won't skunk us.*

The second game becomes the last. We start strong and keep going. Never ahead by much. One point. Two points. Three points. Then tied. Two more points ahead. Our team plays like a well-oiled machine … and somehow, strangely, keeping the lead. At an agonizing snail's pace, never with a big enough margin so you can relax, our players push that second game through to 25-23. And Murray never chokes.

At the end, Tracy, Jamie, Brad, I ... all the parents ... leap up, ecstatic. My God, we're in the finals! Suddenly we can't get less than second. Good Lord, for sure we'll get a silver medal! How great is that!!!

One more match to go. What have we got to lose??? Nothing. Hey, we'd all settle for silver, the ninth-place team going home in second place. Not bad. A little guts here, that's all we need, the second-place team making this a respectable final match. This time against California's Balboa Bay #1.

I settled into the bleachers of the Stadium Court, seven rows up, one of several thousand spectators. Turning to another Riptides mother, I said, "I just don't want them to blow us away in two. Last year the finals were a joke—over in twenty minutes. We've gotta do better than that."

She said, "You're right. We have to make it a contest."

To my amazement, we start out ahead. And then it happens again. Point by point, often tied, never ahead by more than one or two, we eke out the first game. Grinning madly, I turn to the Riptides mom. "Well, it won't be a slaughter. Balboa will have to take it to three."

She laughs. "Not bad for the finals."

The second game of that match is agony. I'm bent over, leaning into my knees, breathing in spurts, hardly able to watch. Balboa Bay has put their two tallest blockers on Dane, taking away his massive kills, rendering him ineffective at net. But he's saving balls in the back court. And Murray, with nobody blocking him, is blasting away the ball. Never missing. And we're slowly accumulating points. One by one. Not a lead you can count on. But a lead. A teeny, weenie, miniscule, gorgeous lead.

Toward the end Balboa takes us to a 23-all tie. And then we win two more points. And suddenly the match is over. We've won the gold!

Bedlam erupted on the court. All of us rushed down, and now everybody was hugging everybody else. I hugged Dane, I hugged the other players, I hugged the coach, I hugged Tracy, I hugged Jamie. I practically hugged the net poles. What's not to hug?

Ten minutes later, the three winning teams stood on the podium to get their medals. The camera flashes never stopped. And then they announced the all-tournament team, starting with Riptides. Murray and one other player were mentioned, but not Dane. I didn't dare look at Tracy. How unfair was this!! The naming of the all-tournament players went on, and Tracy and I both knew that, somehow, Dane had been passed over. We'd seen it happen before. Well, now it had happened again. The edge went off the day.

Finally, the all-tournament team was complete. And Dane wasn't on it.

But wait—one last announcement remained, a choice made by all the top couches in the tournament. In a calm, authoritative voice that seemed to come from On High, the emcee said, "And now for the Most Valuable Player of the 2009 Junior Olympics ... Dane Worley!!"

Whatever else happens in life, I will never forget that moment. It will remain in my heart as a pinnacle unlike any other. A collection of words you couldn't change, a triumph nobody could diminish. You would walk away with it. Live with it. Wake up in the middle of the night and remember it. In my heart I was thinking, *Dane, you did more than make the all-tournament team. You've given me bragging rights for the rest of my life.*

As a postscript, the UCLA coach found Dane, and together, the two beamed and discussed his future. Another UCLA recruit asked for Dane's jersey. And I found myself telling Rob long distance, If the team hadn't gutsed it out the way they did—all of them, and Murray especially—that MVP would have gone to somebody else. It wasn't just Dane's victory. The plaque belonged to The Riptides. To all of them.

I only hoped the SC coach was there to see it.

Now that Tracy was once again married and her family succeeding, she could move on to activities she'd once enjoyed full-out: Tennis and eventually the new sport of Pickleball.

Chapter Twenty-Three

A Classroom Beckons Again

Life moved on for me, too. With our four remaining children grown, and all but our youngest, Kirk, well-established in careers, I doubled-down on my writing, always intent on selling *Higher Than Eagles*, yet still producing other books, beyond the four romances I co-authored with my favorite writing partner, Betty-Jo.

How well I remember the two of us, back then, sitting in one living room or the other, giggling over sex scenes and vowing, "We'll make them warm but not crude. We'll never use the words, 'his throbbing member.'"

By then, our second-son, Chris, was an orthopedic surgeon, our fourth, Kenny, was a lawyer in Virginia, and Tracy had earned an MBA ... put to use in several important projects outside the home, such as setting up a cardiovascular lab.

In 1985, I once again became a teacher. But this time it was almost accidental, and it involved adults instead of children. Pat Kubis, my mentor and writing teacher at Orange Coast College, suddenly found herself with an overlarge student enrollment. One day, knowing I'd been published by Harlequin, she said, "Maralys, my current class is overflowing. How would you like to form a new class and take the romance writers?"

Kubis had no way of knowing she'd just fulfilled one of my private, unspoken dreams. *If I ever get published*, I told myself, *I'd like to teach others*. Suddenly there I was, with a teaching job that fell into my lap.

Rob's response was typical. "You might as well take it, Babe. You're always lecturing, anyway."

When, in 1990, Orange Coast College decided it couldn't support two creative writing teachers, I moved on to a new teaching job at North Orange County Community College … where I've been ever since.

In subsequent years, nearly all the romance writers I'd taught earlier at Orange Coast College were eventually published.

However, from then on, almost none of my students were interested in that genre.

As I'd hoped, I never tire of sharing the fascinating tidbits I've since learned about the craft. Years of examining student manuscripts have highlighted small mistakes made by a majority of amateur writers—bits of mischief whose elimination can make a profound difference in the work's overall quality.

Of course my class varies with each new semester. A few students leave and others join. But interesting to me, students who've long ago left often unexpectedly return.

Our format is that of a glorified critique group, meaning each student edits the work of everyone else, while I point out ways to improve the writing. Because I'm a fairly loosey-goosey teacher, there's this prevailing sense that *we're all in this together.*

Still, because conflict anywhere except in your own life is always enticing, several students remain in memory. Among them was the man whose ego could not stand the success of other students. His critiques were harsh—but only for one set of writers … those whom the class considered praiseworthy. It didn't take long for the other students to notice. From then on, they simply ignored his comments.

Perhaps most memorable was the woman lawyer whose memoir concerned an accident suffered in Mexico—and her subsequent stint in a Mexican jail.

The problem was, while driving along a Mexican highway at night, she had accidentally killed a male pedestrian. As usually happens in a memoir, the writer's attitude quickly surfaced. The woman didn't have a speck of sympathy for the man she'd killed. We all kept trying to convince her … "Even if you don't care about the man, Dorothy," we said, "you'd better fake it. Without some glimmer of humanity, you don't come off looking good. No reader will care about you, or what happened afterward."

But Dorothy was tough and hard-bitten. She didn't waste a moment's thought on the plight of the dead man. And that was that. None of us ever convinced her to modify her attitude. Quite soon, getting nowhere with any of us, she quit the class.

The third category of unwelcome students are those who come to class with their manuscripts finished ... but over the semester, pay no attention to our critiques, continuing to submit chapters which contain the same old mistakes. Privately, one or more students will say to me, "I'm not going to read his stuff any more. He hasn't learned a thing."

But these non-compliant students are so rare as to be unimportant. In contrast, we've all witnessed returning writers who began as rank amateurs and eventually became near-professionals.

These students, as well, soon become obvious to their peers. Many deserved to be published. But the problem today is that publishing leans so heavily on an author's national reputation, that only a few have ever succeeded in finding a traditional publisher.

FOURTEEN YEARS AFTER I FIRST WROTE *HIGHER THAN EAGLES*, AND after endless large and small revisions, I finally sold the manuscript to Longstreet Press. In my head, the celebration went on forever. When I at last dared ask the editor when she decided to buy it, she said, "It was during that clumsy fight between your husband and son in the family room—when they broke the plate-glass window. It was so honest." Ever since, during lectures about memoir-writing, I've emphasized the importance of honesty.

The immediate feedback was gratifying. Within a few years, the book received five movie options, including from Disney and Finnegan-Pinchuk, the producers of *Northern Exposure*. While Disney created a script so silly I was just as glad it was never produced, Finnegan-Pinchuk, in their first attempt, never came up with anything.

And then came the scenario which became, for me, one of life's biggest, most gut-wrenching regrets. Several years after their option expired,

Finnegan-Pinchuk came back again, this time with the news that they'd given the book to an important Hollywood script writer, a woman who loved it and wanted to take on the project.

Unfortunately, by then the script had been optioned again. With that, lawyers for both camps jumped into a protracted, back-and-forth legal fight over movie "rights." By the time the issue was settled, the special screen writer had moved on to another project. For purposes of my story, she was simply gone. I couldn't help feeling bitter that the project was killed by lawyers.

What it meant, long term, was that my book was never sold to Hollywood. Yet even today, everyone who reads it makes the same comment. "This should be a movie."

As a writing teacher, I'm sometimes asked to consider write-for-hire projects, usually by someone who wants to publish his memoir. Only twice have I taken on such a project. The first came from a doctor with a fascinating story about working on a dangerous, commercial fishing boat in Alaska.

Departing from a mundane title, Rob re-named it *Coldwater Kills*. And indeed, the story was gripping. But always an impatient man, long before we'd completed the re-writes, the doctor began submitting it to editors. Unfortunately, in its imperfect state, the manuscript received only rejections. With zero patience to complete the process, the man soon gave up—leaving me regretful that an excellent story had so needlessly been shortchanged … meaning it was never seen by what might have been a rapt audience.

Sadly, the doctor's career in the larger medical world didn't fare much better. Impatience, and a lack of needed preparation played havoc with his practice … one more arena where personality traits can play a larger than expected role.

My only other paid writing venture involved two strangers … young lawyers who came to me with a fascinating story about the death of

President Kennedy. I can only surmise they found me from my then-agent, Patricia Teal. To me, the story is so intriguing it bears repeating.

The manuscript was about a Native American who lived in a gun-steeped state—say, Tennessee—a man known by all the locals as a gifted sharpshooter. To the Indian's surprise, several strange individuals, declaring they represented the U.S. government, sought him out, promising a large reward if he'd consent to a forthcoming shooting assignment.

Reluctantly, the sharpshooter agreed.

Months later, those same odd men found him again and transported him to Dallas. There, in a motel in which he met fellow temporary residents, Lee Harvey Oswald and Jack Ruby, he waited for the assignment.

To his horror, the target was President Kennedy.

During his moments in the book repository, noting details which could only be relayed by someone who'd been there, the Indian waited for the passing of Kennedy's motorcade.

Repulsed by the assignment, the Indian chose to aim high, so his shots would miss the intended target. Unseen by investigators who quickly swarmed the building, the Native American escaped unnoticed.

Only a few years later, the man was jailed for something else. Near death, he related his story, in vivid detail, to a cellmate. My two authors accidentally found themselves interviewing the Indian's cellmate. Fascinated, they taped the story—every detail—then did further research in Texas and wrote a crude script, which they brought to me.

Among the "facts" they came across in Texas (and here I digress), were "generally accepted" scandals about Lyndon Banes Johnson and his questionable early background ... how he exerted his influence to cover-up the unexpected death of a suitor of one of his daughters.

All such tidbits corroborated the Indian's version of events.

After I'd finished editing the script, the authors took it to a permanent repository in Dallas, expressly created for stories and facts relating to the death of Kennedy. There, my authors were told, "This is the most credible account we've yet seen about this event." Excited, the two men relayed this evaluation back to me.

Yet sadly, my authors never convinced a publisher to take the manuscript. I wish now I'd taken the time to make my own copy.

Supposedly, the truth about the Kennedy assassination was long ago finalized as the deed of lone killer Oswald. Yet I've always wondered why Oswald was so quickly and conveniently murdered by Jack Ruby … which meant the *real* truth, if different than it seemed, could never surface in court.

To my surprise, the Kennedy saga has recently re-surfaced with the publication of long-suppressed documents. Among them is a written statement from J. Edgar Hoover: "We've got to convince them this was the work of only one shooter."

From that, the never-convinced public can now speculate once more about the reality behind Kennedy's death.

YEARS AGO, A PROMINENT PHYSICIAN ASKED ME TO WRITE HIS memoir. Rob and I were fascinated by this Chinese doctor's life-story, both here, in China, and in Las Vegas (where he was a professional gambler). I almost agreed. But then I gathered he'd been involved in several ongoing litigations.

I went to the courthouse and looked him up. Sure enough, the doctor had been the plaintiff or defendant in no fewer than eleven lawsuits. Fearing I might become involved in a similar scenario, I declined. Even his unusually generous offer—$25,000—was not worth taking that chance.

ROB'S MOTHER WAS ONCE FOND OF REPEATING A FAVORITE QUIP: "Enough about me. What do YOU think of my recent movie?" This section cannot be concluded without two stories that center on Rob and me—but mostly him. One is scary, the other singular even in today's loony world.

CHAPTER TWENTY-FOUR

Serious Enough for the Mayo Clinic

FOR A NUMBER OF YEARS ROB WAS PLAGUED BY STRANGE MEDICAL symptoms, among them hypoglycemia—which produced weakness, plus a noticeable weight gain.

In 2000, Rob's local endocrinologist finally figured out that something was wrong with Rob's pancreas ... though none of the local surgeons had seen enough such cases to deal with it. Thus Rob was referred to the Mayo Clinic.

Parts of this story are related in an earlier memoir, *A Clown in the Trunk*. Among those moments not mentioned was the hassle of getting to Mayo. Though surgery was scheduled for a Friday in August, the require-ment for Thursday workups meant he needed to arrive in Minnesota late Wednesday—the last leg being a short flight from Chicago to Rochester.

For weather reasons, our plane made a stop elsewhere in Illinois. After three hours sitting on the tarmac, it became clear Chicago's O'Hare could no longer accept our flight or any other; a mid-summer storm had closed it down.

After we made Rob's predicament clear to American Airlines, they hired a van that drove us, and several others, straight through the night and right to the Mayo Clinic. We cannot imagine such a solution happening today. But the incident scared us away, forever, from scheduling other trips through weather-prone Chicago.

As to the surgery, itself: Rob was in the operating room for what seemed like most of a day—so long that I began pacing the hospital halls, unable to hold back tears. By the time he was wheeled back to his room, I was almost incoherent with fear … then overjoyed to have him back.

Later, I learned he'd had his own moments of pure terror. As he was coming out of anesthesia, they rinsed out his air passages with water, meaning for long seconds he felt he was drowning, unable to breathe.

We soon heard the good news. His tumor was on the tail of the pancreas, the part that a patient can lose without serious consequences. While the surgeon was there, he was forced to remove Rob's spleen, but also opted to extract the parathyroids.

Once home, Rob was 25 pounds lighter and no longer weak.

Another bit of amazing news—his sojourn at St. Mary's hospital, almost eleven days in the Intensive Care Unit, tended by full-fledged RNs, cost our insurance company $64,000—a relatively low price for that length and level of care. In the same era, one of our friends back home in California paid nearly $40,000 for an overnight hospital stay.

IT MUST HAVE BEEN DURING ROB'S PRE-MAYO DAYS THAT, DURING A short vacation at the Hyatt Hotel in Poipu, Kauai, he managed to create a stir which some of us, and a few spectators, will never forget.

Because our family made full use of the hotel's pools and water slides, a couple of family members persuaded Rob to try the water slide.

The problem was, the slide was mostly hidden inside a kind of tunnel, where nobody could adequately respond to any kind of mishap. Thus when Rob disappeared up top, he *really* disappeared. For what seemed an inordinately long time our leader-in-chief seemed to have departed from the area.

Anxiously we all waited at the bottom for him to reappear. For the longest time no Rob. But then somebody noticed that the flow of water coming down the slide had also vanished. Nobody could imagine what might be taking place up there, out of sight.

At last, to our surprise, here came Rob. But not in the usual manner. Instead of flowing nicely downward on a moving ribbon of water, he was paddling, and I mean paddling hard, literally pushing himself down the slide with both arms. He was working so hard he was red in the face and sweating.

Down below, the family began to laugh. Rob looked like some brand of animal, a dog, perhaps, pushing himself along the sidewalk to scratch his rear. Instead of the swimmer's usual frolic riding a heavenly stream, Rob's unfortunate breadth meant he had dammed up the flow, so the water then piled up uselessly behind him. Beneath him, the slide was nearly dry.

When he reached the bottom, the collected water gushed out, literally drenching him. Around the edges, the family was convulsed with laughter.

But not Rob. He climbed out of the pool, aggravated and embarrassed. It took a few hours before our leader could fully appreciate the hilarity he'd created for the rest of us.

Needless to say, that was Rob's one and only trip, ever, down the Hyatt's water slide.

SHORTLY AFTER ROB RETURNED FROM THE MAYO CLINIC, WE LOST the last of his parents—both of whom had lived through the depression, but since then had been active members of our family—almost forever, it seemed.

CHAPTER TWENTY-FIVE

Aloha, Art and Ruth

LATE IN THEIR LIVES, ROB'S FATHER, ART, AND HIS MOTHER, RUTH, moved out of the San Fernando Valley and into an apartment near us in Orange County. Now retired, Art found reasons to come visit, and then to plant vegetables and tomatoes in our backyard … and sometimes Ruth joined him up there, either weeding or hoeing. Finally a neighbor asked, "Who are those old people working in your yard?"

"We don't ask them to do it," Rob and I chorused, "they come here because they want to."

For years Ruth's clunky, bright blue Cadillac would arrive in our driveway, followed by various kids yelling, "Granny's here!" and then a stampede to the car … and inevitably, Ruth handing out big and little gifts.

FOR ART'S 90TH BIRTHDAY, THE FAMILY GATHERED ON OUR BACK patio, with the kids and grandkids insisting that the moment was memorable enough to deserve a chocolate cake dotted with a full ninety candles.

The moment they were lit, the cake practically exploded. Flames soared upward, and Art had to duck to avoid being swept into the inferno. Only with massive ingenuity did the younger family members manage to extinguish the flames.

Afterwards, the family, and even Art, joined in relieved laugher—though I'm not sure the cake was edible.

TWO YEARS LATER, ART DIED, AND RUTH WAS LEFT ALONE IN THE apartment. Rob and I visited often, but not as frequently as she deserved. One night Ruth got stuck in her own bathtub and couldn't get out. Now, when it became obvious she could not continue to live unattended, I tried to move her to an assisted-living home. How well I recall her fingers digging into my arm as we drove to view such a residence, and the sound of her crying out in terror, "Nooo! . . Noooo!"

Sympathizing with her fears, I instead hired two kind women who managed, between them, to give her 24-hour care. When at last even home care was insufficient, she moved briefly into a full-care facility.

Those two magnificent women, who'd both cared for her so ardently, now stopped often to visit.

Still graphic in memory is the day Chris and I leaned over her bed, while Ruth, at the moment nearly unconscious and near death, allowed two of us to pipette into her mouth little sips of Boost. We were gratified that she reflexively swallowed.

"She's got to eat something," I said, and Chris nodded, but said, "I'm not sure she wants it."

Yet a few day later, when Christy and Brandon stopped by to visit, Ruth sat up in bed and, like a stage actress, regaled her great-grandchildren with jokes and quips, even poking fun of her own hair, which unaccountably had never grayed, but remained black through her early nineties. Dismayed by its color and lack of curl, she'd bought a series of stylish gray wigs, which she wore without fail.

But not that day.

"Oh, I look terrible," she lamented, "without my wig I look terrible, don't look at me!" bemoaning the fact that for the moment her gray wig was elsewhere.

As Christy said later, "It was the first time I ever saw her without it."

The two kids stared at her, entranced.

Later the conversation veered in another direction. "I'm a queen," she said, "and we're all part of the same royal family. So let's rub noses," for which the kids leaned over her bed … for the moment ignoring the fact that such a ritual is primarily associated with Eskimos.

For Ruth, this was indeed a last, royal performance. Later Christy said, "Granny Ruth was always funny, but Brandon and I found that day she was in rare form."

Two days later, she died.

IT WAS LUCKY ROB WASN'T THERE WHEN RUTH'S GRANDKIDS dismantled her apartment. Like pillagers, they tore into her possessions, holding up a scarf or purse or towel. "Anybody want this?" they asked, and after a moment of silence, "Out it goes—into Goodwill." More often, the item hit the trash.

Rob would have protested every move, fought for each usable item. Yet even I, not the pack rat that Rob has become, was horrified at their speed, at how fast they dispensed with everything, even brand new items. Sometimes I balked.

"Mom, you don't want a corset," Tracy said.

"But it's brand new. Never been worn."

"Who you going to find to take it?" my daughter asked. "Nobody. Women don't wear corsets any more. So out it goes."

After the first day of plunder, Chris went to the apartment that evening with Betty-Jo, and operating on a hunch, he began lifting piles of washcloths, of table linens, of gloves or hats. And under nearly every one he found small stacks of twenty dollar bills.

"Look, Betty-Jo—more money!"

His search continued, until Betty-Jo finally exclaimed in exasperation, "Come on, Chris, you've found everything! There can't be any more."

"Gotta look a little further," he said, and sure enough, he found yet more stacks of carefully-hidden bills.

Finished at last, he came to our house, exuberant over his treasure hunt. "Count it, Dad!" he said. "Just look at how much money I found! She had it stacked everywhere."

And Rob did count it. Chris's pile amounted to over six-thousand dollars.

"Mom was hiding it from Art," Rob said. "She never trusted that her husband would provide her with enough money. She knew he was traumatized by being one of five boys raised in straitened circumstances. And later by the Depression, which was even worse. With her, Art was always pretty tight."

"It's odd," I said. "Despite his frugality, he was always generous with us."

"And us, too," Chris said, then added, "Can't believe all the places Granny stashed it away. Like a rat, she had droppings everywhere."

"That's my mom," said Rob. "She always had a semi-secret life that Art never knew about."

Within two days, Ruth's grandchildren had dispensed with everything. A new mattress. Never-used hats. Pots and pans. Linens.

I sat and stared, aware that the whole process was both fast and you might say, "ruthless." In my heart of hearts, I knew that someday, which I hoped was far off, that same speedy, unsentimental process would take place in our home … that our kids and grandkids would toss away most of the "stuff" we'd spent a lifetime accumulating.

The mental image of those two days will be forever stark in my mind's eye, a prognosticator of similar days to come.

Chapter Twenty-Six

The Anti-Choke Squad

By coincidence, two of our sons have utilized the Heimlich maneuver to save someone's life. The first occurred in a hospital, when Chris was made aware that a nearby doctor was choking. Unable to speak, the physician backed up to Chris and gestured for him to do the maneuver. Chris obliged—until something popped out of the victim's mouth. It was then Chris learned that his colleague had been choking on a piece of See's Candy.

A comedian drawn to dark humor might add, "What a way to go!"

The second event was more complicated. For the first time, our fourth son, Kenny, had invited a particular fellow lawyer and wife to his Norfolk, Virginia, home for dinner. His wife, Melanie, always the consummate hostess, had cooked delicious roasted lamb chops. "I believed my job was to wow them," she said, so she made a five-course meal.

Ken, who loves lamb chops, was concentrating on his plate when the other lawyer, a somewhat overweight man, reached for some wine, took a sip, and, according to Melanie, "It just came back on the table." She noticed a startled look on the man's face. Immediately the lawyer jumped up and left the room, with his wife and Melanie quickly following. The two ladies were on either side, holding him up.

Since Kenny was faced in the opposite direction, he said, "Call me if you need me."

Within seconds Melanie shouted, "Kenny, we need you!" Then she called to her daughter, Juliette, then eleven, "Call 911."

"He's choking!" she cried to Ken. Even as she said it, Melanie was trying to grab him for the Heimlich maneuver, but to no avail. He was too heavy, and he was rapidly sinking to the floor.

Quickly Kenny arrived. By then the victim's eyes had started to roll to the back of his head, he was turning blue, and drool dripped from his mouth … which the wife kept wiping with a cloth napkin.

With that, Kenny lifted the man off the ground and from behind, he began the Heimlich maneuver.

Kenny's first five or six thrusts failed to dislodge whatever was in his colleague's trachea. All the while he was aware that time was of the essence. Lacking oxygen for more than two minutes, the man would surely suffer brain damage.

At last Kenny gathered every ounce of energy and exerted a thrust that he feared would shatter the other's sternum.

With that, the meat flew out of the man's mouth—and to Melanie's surprise, the wife caught it in her napkin. To her further surprise, the object was now shaped like a hot dog.

To everyone's relief, the guest once again began breathing. For a moment, the two couples just stood there, so overwhelmed that none of them knew what to say. It was obvious Kenny had just averted a tragedy.

Right then Melanie remembered that Juliette was still talking to 911. She ran to the kitchen, said, "I'll take over, honey," and told the 911 operator the crisis was resolved. At which the operator on the other end said, "Your daughter was so polite. She kept saying, 'Yes, Ma'am, and no, Ma'am.'"

"Well, that's nice," said Melanie, but privately she was thinking, *Juliette just didn't realize how bad the situation was.*

Strangely, the four all sat down on the living room sofas and sipped coffee—making small talk that had nothing to do with the elephant in the room.

Not knowing what else to suggest, Melanie asked weakly, "Can I get you all some dessert?"

The other couple shook their heads. "I think … " the wife paused, "I think we'd better be going." And indeed, Melanie noticed the man's suit front was a mess.

In near silence, Ken and Melanie walked the other couple to their car. As the vehicle started to pull away, it stopped, and the man rolled down his window. In a voice of embarrassment, he said to Kenny and Melanie, "If I ever do that again, my wife says she'll kill me!"

Laughter all around seemed to relieve the tension.

The next time Melanie saw the lawyer, he'd lost weight, about forty pounds, she decided. Both Ken and Melanie understood what the weight loss was all about. Their lawyer friend had opted to improve his health and avoid another such crisis.

ON A WHOLLY DIFFERENT NOTE, KENNY REGALED US WITH ANOTHER of those moments that could only happen to him.

To set the stage: years earlier, in college at UCLA, he was on the swim team, a star competitor, but especially in his specialty, the butterfly. In his sophomore year he narrowly missed qualifying for the Olympics. As noted earlier, the athletes he competed with, swimming on either side of him in the prelims, were destined to win medals in the 1976 Montreal Olympics.

Now, in his late forties, Ken and Melanie attended a swim meet at the Norfolk Yacht and Country Club, where their daughters were on the team.

At the meet's intermission, the league's teams traditionally held adult relays … a swim-off between the visiting team coaches and friends, and those aligned with the club.

In this case, the visiting team's adult men were mostly athletes still in their twenties—very fit swimmers who had recently competed, or were still competitive swimmers.

Not so with the Norfolk Yacht club adults who, as years-ago college competitors, were mostly in their late forties. To Ken's surprise he was suddenly conscripted to compete on his local team. Several problems arose. Most important, he hadn't brought a swim suit. Not to be dissuaded, he accepted the loan of somebody's baggy shorts, which were not only a tad too big, but bound to be a negative influence when it came to moving quickly through water.

Concerned that the shorts might actually fall off, he cast about for a solution—which turned out to be somebody handing him a length of rope. With that, he secured the floppy shorts to his body. Furthermore, the group assigned Kenny as relay anchor, in what was known as a sprint relay.

When Ken dove into the pool, his relay team, miraculously, was tied with the much-younger team. It turned out that both anchors went in together.

For the whole length of the pool, Ken swam all-out, for once without taking a breath. At the end, he out-touched the anchor on the other team by split seconds.

Watching him, Melanie and the other wives broke into cheers. For Kenny, for the whole family, the relay proved to be a moment of great, unexpected victory.

The younger swimmers could not believe what had happened. Finally, one was heard to ask, "Who was the old guy with the rope?"

FOR NOW, THIS IS THE LAST OF THE STORIES ABOUT OUR OWN children. As promised, the next few chapters concern grandkids—who have a way of growing up, so that I, for one, am apt to forget which generation they belong to.

CHAPTER TWENTY-SEVEN

The Next Generation Adds New Luster

As Rob so often proclaims, I'm always lecturing. One of my parenting riffs to mothers suggests that writing down what the child says is nearly as important as taking pictures. In later years, parents tend to remember with delight some of their children's truly fetching comments.

Within past pages are some of the memorable comments I've recalled from my parents, grandparents, and our own children. From here on, most of this book will be devoted to statements and yes, vignettes involving both grandchildren and great-grandchildren.

For some, this section can't come soon enough. Two of my great grandchildren, both determined to be authors and now seeking their own 15 minutes of fame, frequently ask, "*When are you going to write about me?*"

As old photos tend to be gathered up and displayed haphazardly, so too, this text will now do some loose jumping around.

One of my first memories about a new grandchild still remains a vivid, mental imagine. The year was 1977, when our second grandchild, Christy, became the first child of Betty-Jo and our son, Chris. At the time the family lived in New Jersey, while Chris commuted to New York and NYU medical school.

One night while Rob and I were visiting, Chris came home from school, placing his briefcase on the floor. Christy, perhaps just over age one—delicate in build with filmy blonde hair—decided to explore its contents. What struck me as remarkable was that she'd figured out how, by

159

pressing a certain button, she could snap open one side. But then, as we watched, she crawled to the OTHER side and pushed that button as well—grasping that it took more than one maneuver to get the case unlocked. Even a briefcase can be an I.Q. test.

ANOTHER BRIEF MEMORY CONCERNS TRACY'S DAUGHTER, JAMIE. SHE must have been about five, and for some reason she and I were traveling home on the freeway, just the two of us. But thanks to heavy traffic, we were barely moving. To my dismay—no, exasperation—this went on for some time. Finally Jamie asked, with perfect logic, "Why doesn't the front car go faster?"

I wanted to explain, but she was too young to understand—that the same thing can happen in the sky, when a line of airplanes is forced to slow down due to a kind of progressive back-up called a flow pattern, which affects each plane to a greater degree than the one in front of it.

This also happens in grocery lines, or so it seems.

OUR OLDEST GRANDSON, BRANDON, WAS BORN TO OUR SON, BOBBY, about a month before Christy arrived. I remember getting the call one November night at an hour when nobody wants to pry herself out of a warm bed. Whatever the time, I jumped up ... deciding, as I usually do, that some events are worth the discomfort of losing a night's sleep. Brandon is now 6'3", a modified version of his father, so my memory of his birth is hazy—except I do recall being outside the delivery room and hearing our first grandchild's first cry. For that precious "first" I gladly forfeited sleep.

Sadly, before he was a year old, Brandon's father, Bobby, was killed in that hang gliding accident—leaving Brandon to learn about his famous father in small steps over many years. And also, in my book, *Higher Than Eagles*.

In time his mother, Suzette, remarried a fine man, John, so from then on Brandon had a father figure in his life.

At age twenty-two, Brandon married Rachel, and the two scheduled their wedding reception for our half-acre backyard—ultimately the scene of three family wedding receptions. The couple now have two children, Scarlet and Spencer. (Clearly, their parents favor old movies.)

As an adult, wanting to participate in his father's sport, Brandon took hang gliding lessons, and as reported by the new owners of Wills Wing, "He learned quickly and did well."

Rob and I know Brandon and his wife in many ways, but especially as helpful and entertaining traveling companions. I particularly remember the time Rob and I sat with Brandon and Rachel in a Scottish restaurant, where, typically, I happened to glance at Brandon's plate and saw a morsel that looked interesting. I pointed. "May I have a bite of that?"

"Of course," he said, offering me a spoon. Obviously this had happened many times during our trip. As I took the proffered bite, he said, "Your stomach is now a cornucopia of one-biters." That was just one of the many Brandon-isms that kept me laughing.

CHRIS'S AND BETTY-JO'S DAUGHTER, CHRISTY, WAS BORN A MONTH after Brandon. Our photo albums abound with pictures of the two cousins—Brandon, sturdy, chubby and tall, literally looming over the delicate Christy. Over the years, during family vacations, Christy and Brandon have enjoyed a kind of brother/sister relationship.

In 1989, with Christy just shy of 13, Rob and I took her to England and Scotland. My memory of our first excursion on London's underground was of Christy's hasty review of posted maps and directions, after which her pace increased until she was striding out ahead of us, as though she knew exactly where we were going. "Hurry, Rob, we've gotta catch her," I said, bewildered—until we both realized that she DID know exactly where we were going.

In ensuing days in Wales and Scotland, Rob said, "Look at her—another castle she's exploring on her own."

AS SHE GREW, ALWAYS LIVING WITHIN BLOCKS OF US, CHRISTY AND I enjoyed an unusual relationship, as though she was one of my girlfriends. She recalls a time when the two of us visited a mall, with Christy remarking, "Sometimes my friends and I run up the down escalator." To her astonishment, I said, "Let's us do it," which we did—with me arriving safely on top. To this day she's amazed that her grandmother would try, and even accomplish, such a feat.

As a high school senior, already well-grounded in Spanish, Christy became an exchange student in Honduras, where she lived for six months with a local family and became thoroughly bilingual … a skill which later became invaluable.

In time Christy graduated from U.C. Berkeley, and soon was accepted in Berkeley's Boalt Hall, preparing to become a lawyer. As a family we rejoiced, knowing that even the acceptance to that law school was an honor. Later, law degree in hand, and with her aptitude in Spanish, Christy became a Public Defender.

Sometime after graduation, we learned that Christy had met Mike Pierce, a graduate of University of Vermont. One day they came to our house to visit. As he sat on our family room sofa, Rob asked, "Mike, where do you see yourself in five years?"

Mike answered casually, "Wherever Christy is," which Rob noted as an unusual, perhaps less than laudatory, goal. But Mike's words became prophetic. Soon the two exchanged vows in the grassy field of Chris's new ranch, where our daughter, Tracy, officiated—with her two-day ministerial role procured especially for the wedding.

YEARS LATER, WITH THE TWO NOW LIVING IN OAKLAND, CHRISTY became pregnant with twins. One night when Mike was, as always, running his new restaurant, Maverick, in San Francisco, Christy eased herself down in their bathtub. But suddenly she was faced with a dilemma: in her advanced stage of pregnancy she couldn't get out. And Mike wasn't due home for hours. Nor did she have a nearby cell phone to call for help.

With that, she thought if she drained the tub, she might increase her ability to maneuver. But no such luck. By then she'd gained more than 50% of her body weight. To start, she'd been 107 pounds, but now at this advanced stage, she was 165 pounds, and was, as she described it, "almost square."

For awhile she lay there helpless, contemplating solutions which had no chance of working.

At last, she was somehow able to pull a towel in with her, then to roll over on her knees—a remarkable feat, as she hadn't seen her knees, much less her feet, in months. The maneuver took enormous strength and willpower. With the towel adding a modicum of security to the slippery bottom, and using more muscles than seemed reasonable, she was able, eventually, to stand.

Needless to say, that was her last, pre-birth soak in a tub.

Some time later, Christy parked her car in a parking garage—only to learn when she returned that a new car had parked on the driver's side—so close, in her enlarged state, that she couldn't open the door wide enough to get in. Aware that many cars in the structure belonged to movie-goers, she realized it would be futile to stand there and wait—lest the owner be gone for several more hours.

Instead, she tried to figure out a new means of reaching her seat on the driver's side—in a car that happened to be the original, tiny Prius.

Finally the car on the passenger side left, leaving her enough room to enter through the wrong door. With great difficulty she hoisted herself over the center console, and finally into the driver's seat.

A few months later she gave birth to fraternal twin girls, Marley and Malena—eleven pounds worth of baby and different from each other in every way.

THE LIFE OF CHRIS'S SECOND DAUGHTER, KELLY, TOOK AN ENTIRELY different trajectory. Enrolled in U.C. Davis, Kelley earned an engineering degree with a double major, in both mechanical and aeronautical engineering. Almost immediately she was offered an engineering position by the Navy. For some years she has gone on Naval training missions, for the purpose of testing Sea Sparrow missiles.

Before long, to her father's delight, Kelly earned a pilot's license and was now able to fly Chris's planes. Together, the two sometimes went to out-of-state fly-ins.

Married to a long-time boyfriend, Matt—a computer expert—she eventually had a boy, Oliver, then a girl, Nora.

As her children grew able to cope, the family acquired two vigorous huskies. My favorite memory of Kelly is when she popped the two young kids—then two and four—in a kind of funky wheeled carriage, harnessed up the dogs, and ran behind the craft, guiding them for several miles as the huskies pulled the kids along sidewalks. With nearby drivers doing startled double-takes, Kelly eventually completed her local version of the Iditarod, arriving at her parents' house, some 2 ½ miles away.

BETTY-JO AND CHRIS'S THIRD CHILD, LAUREN, FOLLOWED AN entirely different course than her older sisters. Long before her career was established, she married Dan, a restaurant manager, and within a few years had a boy, Corbin, then a girl Annalise. With an early job as an assistant to a hospital pharmacist, and a stint as a Doula, (birthing assistant,) she'd long worked around hospitals.

Intent on moving up the healthcare ladder, and now as a mother with young children, Lauren eventually entered nursing school, became an RN and soon achieved a regular hospital job. From there she acquired an additional degree in Hospice Care—which she finds both humane and satisfying.

Lauren is now about to start a Nursing Master's program.

As she headed home from our area—on one of her mid-winter trips up Highway 50 to her house in Lake Tahoe, Lauren became the central figure in a drama which I wrote up and sent out as a blog. Ultimately, it was read by nearly 3000 people. The story, written a couple of years ago, reads as follows:

TRAGEDY ON HIGHWAY 50

I FIRST LEARNED OF THE EVENT WHEN MY DAUGHTER-IN-LAW, Betty-Jo, said, "Have you heard what happened to Lauren on the way home?"

"What? What?" My heart started racing. Just the day before—the Tuesday after Christmas—my granddaughter, Lauren, and her two small children had flown to Sacramento, then driven up the mountain to their home in South Lake Tahoe.

Betty-Jo added quickly, "Lauren's okay. She and the kids are fine."

And then she told most of the story ... and the rest came from Lauren.

Near midnight, as they headed into the Sierras, Lauren noticed strange lights in the distance, but off Highway 50, and down near the American River. She thought, *That house down there has awfully bright lights.*

Only seconds later, figures standing on the shoulder were flagging her down. Lauren pulled off and stopped. They were on a winding, two-lane mountain road, miles from anywhere. She noticed the car thermometer read 30 degrees.

As she got out, her children started protesting. Annalise, two, and Corbin, three, were strapped into their seats ... and didn't like her leaving.

A man—someone from one of the first cars on the scene—said urgently, "That's a car down there. Upside down on the edge of the river—partly in the water. With a family inside. We went down, but couldn't get them out. A girl was ejected." His lower pant legs were wet. "Not sure what to do." He seemed frozen, both literally and figuratively.

Lauren is a nurse. She quickly grasped a need—that someone had to take charge. "We have to get them out of that water and up here," she said. She was thinking, *Hypothermia.* Her children were now screaming. But down near the river, someone else was screaming.

"Go down and bring that person up," she ordered.

"How?" the man asked.

"Use this blanket. Put the girl on it, and haul her up. Like a sled." She tossed him a blanket.

By now other cars had been flagged down. People milled around—most of them baffled. "Call 911," she ordered. People tried, but found their phones didn't work.

Odd as it seemed, her phone did. She reached an emergency station, and at midnight, with GPS, gave the dispatcher an approximate location.

"You … Go down the hill and help," she ordered a man who was standing by.

To others she shouted, "Help him pull the blanket." And to still others, "Bring us more blankets. And spare jackets. We'll need them." And to still others, "We need more hands. We've got four accident victims down there."

She shouted herself hoarse, demanding action, putting more men to work pulling the "sleds."

The first to come up was the screamer, a thirteen-year-old girl with a probable broken shoulder. She'd been lying on the hillside and now couldn't move her arm. "What's your name?" Lauren asked.

"Topaz."

"Here, Topaz, get in my car. The heater's on." Lauren began tugging off the girl's damp clothes, then wrapping her in blankets and jackets. Meanwhile, both Annalise and Corbin were still crying.

Next came a woman, twenty-two, with a bloody hand. To escape the car, the woman had punched out the window. In a halting voice she explained she'd found a pocket of breathable air. Lauren could see she was drifting in and out of consciousness. "Climb into my car, in back. What is your name?"

"Bailey." But the victim was dazed, couldn't remember where she was, or what day it was. Unlike the girl, she was wet and icy, clear through. Even her hair.

With strength she didn't know she had, Lauren ripped the woman's shirt in half, right where she sat, pulled down wet pants and underwear, and threw them in back. With donated jackets and blankets, she wrapped the woman up. But the patient seemed to be passing out. Determined to keep her awake, Lauren shouted her name over and over. "Bailey! Bailey!" A step that was vital to keeping her alive. Meanwhile, her own kids had begun screaming.

166

As the two accident victims slowly warmed in the car, other rescuers arrived, five men from CalTrans. Immediately grasping the emergency, one directed traffic and four went down to the half-submerged car. With the help of an off duty Sac P.D. officer, the five entered the freezing water, pushed as a group and managed to right the car. At last the men were able to free the driver, who was still alive.

From her position up on the road, Lauren saw a rescuer leaning over a small boy. She learned he was eleven. But the way the rescuer was acting, Lauren guessed the truth. The boy was already dead. *A child,* she thought, *just a child.* For her, the worst of those traumatic moments. The accident had just become a tragedy.

Now with fire department stretchers, the group of men skidded the boy and injured driver up to the road.

Finally, nearly two hours after she stopped, EMTs arrived, plus two ambulances. One ambulance took the injured man away, with intent to connect with a medical helicopter. By calling the hospital later, Lauren learned he'd suffered a broken back.

"Is he dead?" Corbin asked in his small voice.

"They don't send a helicopter for dead people," Lauren said.

Medics from the other ambulance scooped up the young girl and the woman who'd been sitting in Lauren's car … the latter also wearing Lauren's shoes. At the last moment, as an afterthought, barefoot Lauren retrieved her shoes from the ambulance.

At last, by now nearly two a.m., Lauren and her children continued up the road toward home. The next morning, at nine-thirty, Lauren was on the job in her own hospital. In a quiet, private ceremony, one of the hospital staffers who'd heard the news gave her an award.

A day later, after Lauren told Rob and me the entire story over the phone, I said, "I'm so proud of you, Lauren—the way you took charge. And probably saved lives." And I thought how, within the family, she was never the one who ordered other family members around.

In her unassuming way, Lauren answered, "That's just what we do."

CHAPTER TWENTY-EIGHT

At Last ... A Boy!

THE DAY BABY GEOFF ARRIVED AS PART OF THEIR FAMILY BECAME A kind of punctuation mark for Chris and Betty-Jo. Finally their fourth child was a male—and given the name so esteemed by all of us.

I was present when Geoff was born—a peaceful event that Betty-Jo experienced calmly and with no anesthetic ... to me, a remarkable achievement. Yet she takes no credit. "It hurt, yes. But it was never more than I could stand. So I didn't see the point of taking anything."

From the start, Geoff was a warm and loving child. Yet as Betty-Jo and Chris soon discovered, he was far more rambunctious than his three sisters, disinterested in tedious school sessions that required long sits in a chair. Geoff wanted to be away and "doing."

Eventually, as a teenager, he acquired a fast motorcycle, and was soon intrigued by speed and by the skill needed to jump over obstacles. Skillful riding added to his indifference to school, and eventually he entered motorcycle competitions.

Only by strong pressure from his parents did he agree to attend Humboldt State college near Eureka.

Before college began, disaster struck. Geoff was out in the Mojave desert, jumping over sand dunes, when he made a near-fatal error. Instead of clearing a distant hill, he landed short and the motorcycle flipped over, crushing his left elbow. Taken by helicopter to the nearest hospital—the Eisenhower Medical Center in Rancho Mirage—he was told by an orthopedic surgeon on staff that his elbow would never work again. "Your elbow will be frozen," the surgeon said, meaning Geoff faced a lifetime of an elbow fixed in a slightly bent position.

Refusing to accept such an outcome, Chris got on the phone and arranged for an ambulance to bring Geoff back to Orange County.

Soon Chris found two orthopedic surgeons who agreed to do surgery. At first Chris himself did not plan on being part of the team. But at the last minute, guessing that the job would be overwhelming for two men, he changed his mind. With that, the three surgeons began their work.

Using splintered bone from the injury site, plus an assortment of cadaver bones, the three doctors worked seven hours to reconstruct Geoff's elbow. At last, exhausted, the surgeons left the operating theater, not sure they'd succeeded.

But they had. After weeks of healing, then therapy, Geoff once more had an operational elbow. His scarring was extensive, but the limb worked. Chris considers the return of Geoff's arm to normal function one of the highlights of his surgical career.

Geoff never stopped riding motorcycles. But from then on he took fewer chances.

Ultimately he attended college, stopping just short of attaining a degree. With the death of his favorite professor, Geoff left for good. By coincidence, about then he made a remarkable discovery. In nearby Eureka he found a billboard for sale. With a relatively small investment, Geoff was able to buy it—and discovered, to his delight, a small income stream that seemed to require little or no effort. "It's like a slot machine, the way billboards pay off," he said.

As he enlarged his billboard purchases—perhaps because of them—he also found a job in a small print shop run by a man who created business signage. In Chuck Ellsworth, Geoff found an older man who both understood and appreciated his interesting young worker.

Meanwhile, as he acquired more and more such outdoor signage, Geoff didn't seem to be aware that he was *working*. He explained to his father, "I'm getting all this money for doing nothing."

Later, Chris reported to us, "He doesn't seem to notice the effort that is required to purchase, take charge of, and maintain all his billboards."

Eventually, now the owner of a dozen billboards, Geoff was able to buy out his boss's business. Yet even today Chuck has stayed on to help him—an interesting reversal, now that Geoff is technically Chuck's boss.

Soon Geoff married his long-standing girl friend, Amber, in an outdoor ceremony at his parent's ranch in San Diego county.

Geoff has currently parlayed his billboard and signage businesses into a decent enough income so he could afford to build a large house just outside the city limits of Eureka.

One day he held up a greatly-magnified picture of the check that secured his purchase of the signage company. "Here's my college degree," he said with a grin, albeit with a hint of defiance. And indeed, the one child of Betty-jo's and Chris's without a college degree may end up, monetarily, as the most successful.

Geoff and Amber now have two children, a girl, Ella, and a boy, Emmett. Further stories will illustrate that his children come close to being as unusual as their father.

CHAPTER TWENTY-NINE

A Trio of Virginia Belles

ONLY ONE OF OUR CHILDREN RELOCATED TO ANOTHER STATE. OUR fourth son, Kenny, followed a beauty queen to Virginia, passed the State Bar, then married another Virginia beauty, Melanie Koch. They had three daughters—all talented, and no two even vaguely alike. Eventually they moved to an elegant old Norfolk home on the water.

For Rob and me it becomes impossible to forge the same intimate friendships with far-away grandchildren as we enjoy with those closer to home.

Yet I still have varied, if fleeting impressions of each of them. I now recall the time that Isabelle, the tall, willowy middle girl, and I drove to the store near their home. She was then about fifteen. Coming back, I asked, "Now which way do I turn, Isabelle?" And with great confidence she replied, "Next corner, turn right."

As it turned out, right was wrong.

"Oh," she said, giggling, "I guess it's the corner after that."

But her next instruction went astray too. And soon, the less likely it seemed she knew our way back, the more assertive became her directions.

"I know. I know," she said, "it's two more streets. And then you go left." This time she sounded absolutely sure—but *sure* didn't make it. And once more she dissolved in giggles.

For some twenty minutes we wandered *near* but not *in* her neighborhood. And by now I could see this short trip had turned into an adventure. Just as I began to wonder if we'd ever return that day, I recognized a familiar street. And right then she said, "Oh THAT ONE!" And finally she was oriented. But by then she had me laughing, too.

Such confidence, I thought, no matter how wrong she was … combined with laughter at her own mistakes. I'd never had such a good time being lost. Being with Isabelle made the whole scenario memorable—and yes, worthwhile.

Years later, Isabelle graduated from The College of Charleston with a degree in psychology—and Rob and I were lucky enough to be there, witnessing the ceremony. As always since we'd known her, Isabelle was light-hearted and full of fun.

The youngest girl, Juliette, impressed Rob and me from the start with her zeal and warmth when she learned to play the piano. She really pounded out her pieces. At the time, she was the least talkative of the three. I think she eventually gave up her music. But now this talented young woman, dark-haired and also tall, has graduated from the University of North Carolina at Wilmington, and is presently working on an advanced degree leading to a career as a Physician's Assistant.

Interestingly, Tracy's son, Dane, may know Juliette better than any of us here on the West Coast. During long-ago large-family get togethers—in places like Little Dix Bay in the Virgin Islands—those two took a liking to one another. I can still recall Dane, a couple of years older than Juliette and perhaps around nine, lifting her off the ground and carrying her around the lawns. "It's like she's his pet," I said to Rob.

Over the years, their friendship only increased, perpetuated because Dane and Juliette kept emailing each other long distance. "Sometimes the only way we know what's going on with the Ken Wills family is by asking Dane," I remarked to Rob. Even today they remain warm, long-distance buddies. If this holds true, it's partly because Dane has consistently been one of the few males I know who *talks.* And for all us women, that makes Dane both unusual and special.

Ken and Melanie's oldest daughter, Erica, has always been both thoughtful and helpful to her parents. For years, she and the son of their local Presbyterian pastor were close enough so our West Coast family, at

174

least, assumed they would eventually marry. Once, the young man accompanied the family to California—a kind, red-headed lad who was a joy to know.

However, the son went off to a military school and the friendship expired. Petite and blonde, Erica graduated from Marymount University near Washington, D.C.. Having completed a year as a beloved student teacher, she shared with us an enthusiastic notebook that her students put together for her. Soon she moved to Washington, D.C., where she taught first grade.

A year later, she married Christian Carpenter, who, in his senior year at Marymount enlisted in the Marines. As of this writing, they have a boy, a girl, and now a second little girl.

I especially recall the visit to our neighborhood from Erica and her two young children—and how we all had a picnic in a local park, with young Knox gobbling down vegetables as though they were candy. I asked Erica, "How do you get him to eat mashed peas, which most kids would refuse? Kids his age always prefer sweets and empty foods like white crackers."

She smiled. "I've never given him a choice. Vegetables, fruits, and wholesome meats are all I've ever fed him. He doesn't know the difference." She grinned as she held out a teaspoon of spinach … and her son popped open his mouth and accepted it eagerly, like ice cream.

Clearly, Erica has taken on motherhood as a high-calling … a job which suits her loving and sincere personality.

How well we all recall when Christian received his Marine Commission as a Second Lieutenant. The ceremony was held outside, near a flagpole on the Old Dominion University campus. Somehow, Knox got loose, and in the midst of the ceremony, with a Marine Colonel presiding, came running across the commons, holding out his arms, grinning widely, and saying, "Hi, Daddy!" Under our breaths, we spectators giggled.

Christian never changed expression. Somebody scooped up the child, and the commissioning went on.

THANKS TO MY ASKING KEN FOR SOME OF HIS KIDS' CUTE SAYINGS, HE complied with the following list. I may not have heard these pronouncements myself, but for me they have the same impact as if I had.

The following tidbits are from Ken's journal.

KEN'S TITLE: "WHEN OUR KIDS WERE VERY YOUNG"

June, 1993:

Erica, walking with me down a Norfolk street, asked, "Daddy, are you going to live a long time?" I replied that I hoped so, and wondered aloud why she had asked. "Because I want you to walk with me to California."

This summer I was eating out of a carton of ice cream with Erica, and was apparently not sharing enough with her, because she said, "Daddy, you're not being fair to your little daughter."

March, 1994.

A few days ago Erica said to Isabelle: "Did you know that our first President, George Washington, died?" Isabelle asked when, and Erica replied: "Don't worry, it was a long time ago."

April, 1994

In the kitchen the other day, Erica said to us: "When I was two years old, Dad used to give me his root beer. Didn't you, Big Boy?"

November, 1994

We were on a very bumpy flight, heading to California for Thanksgiving, when Isabelle said: "Quick, call Grandma Maralys and tell her we're trying to come see her, but the wind keeps blowing the plane upside down. I hope we don't hit the ground and go Boom." Erica than said, "We need Eskimo suits. They'll keep us from getting hurt if we crash."

February, 1995

Erica asked, "Who made God, and why does God let people die?"

176

Later Isabelle told us she wanted to be a lifeguard so she could "blow the whistle when people drown."

April, 1995

Juliette stuck her tongue out at Erica, who asked her not to do that. Juliette replied that she was "just giving my tongue some fresh air."

July, 1995

As Juliette and I walked home from a funeral reception down the block, she stated that we would all die someday. I said yes but that I hoped it wouldn't be for a long time. She said it was all right, because we would go to heaven and up there we would be angels. She then said that when we were together in heaven she would still scratch my back. Then she paused, and said, "I think I'll scratch your wings instead."

January 23 1996

Juliette told Melanie, "I hear God telling me to go inside and get something to eat."

April, 1996

On Easter morning Juliette came into our bedroom, said, "Happy Easter," and handed us her used diaper. She laughed and so did we. Downstairs, she showed me her new "ring" from her Easter basket, and said, "We're rich, and you're not." She then extended her hand to me and said, "Kiss it."

May, 1997

Erica was at the kitchen pantry and asked me to help her open a box of cereal. I did, and then triumphantly, and kiddingly lifted the box overhead as high as my arms could reach. Erica then said, "Daddy, I asked you to help me open it, not raise it high like it's a newborn king!"

July, 1998

Melanie and Juliette were in the middle of a discussion about sharing some candy. Melanie spotted a particularly large piece—the largest Juliette had—and asked if she could have it. Juliette looked at the candy, then looked at Melanie, then studied the candy. Last she looked Melanie straight in the eye, moved closer so they were almost nose to nose, and said, "Not in your lifetime, Buster."

While I was bringing home several live lobsters from the grocery store with Isabelle, she looked inside the bag holding them and said: "Hello, Mr. Lobster. This is your new owner, Mr. Ken Wills. He's going to torture you."

November, 2000

I have an (unoriginal) expression which I use, in mock hurtfulness, with the kids: "What am I, chopped liver?" The other day Isabelle's response was: "No, you're just liver."

May, 2001

Isabelle, commenting on First Presbyterian Church's new contemporary worship service; "I don't think the service should be such a loud and bouncy kind of thing—I think it should be quiet and holy."

September, 2001

Melanie and the kids were in the car having a general discussion about their classmates taking more candy than they are entitled to from teachers' goody baskets. Isabelle then said, "When I was in 3rd grade, I stole an extra piece of candy, and I was overtaken with grief, and became sick to my stomach and never stole again."

Later, when Juliette was packing for a trip to Wyoming, she showed us a variety of things she was putting in her suitcase and said, "I've got my contraptions, and I'm ready to rumble."

December, 2001

Juliette was sitting at our kitchen table helping Melanie prepare for dinner by snapping green beans. I tickled her once, and then again. With that she said to me, "I've got beans and I'm not afraid to use them."

Also in December, Juliette was telling us that a classmate, Noah, had gotten into some trouble at school by talking. I asked her if talking at school wasn't alright. She replied, "Not if you're doing it 24/7."

FROM THESE COMMENTS, IT'S EASY TO SEE WHAT KIND OF WORLD Ken and Melanie provided for their children. Also, it seems that Juliette Wills was particularly keen on using smart-alec adult vernacular … while both Isabelle and Erica were imbued with a strong inner sense of morality.

As a mirror for those fleeting early years with children, I can only wish that more parents wrote down the memorable things that their young children said.

LUCKY FOR US, WE LIVED CLOSE ENOUGH TO A FEW OF OUR GRANDKIDS to hear them describe the big moments in their lives.

CHAPTER THIRTY

The Drama Runs Both Ways

AT LAST JAMIE GRADUATED FROM CAL POLY SAN LUIS OBISPO, having found in landscape architecture a perfect outlet for her creativity. Yet even with that degree, she wasn't qualified to sign off on landscape plans. Instead, all graduates were required to work in the field for a minimum of three years before they qualified to take the national exams.

For those requisite years, Jamie was apprenticed to a landscape architect with such dazzling contacts she found herself sitting in the home of Elon Musk. Though he'd commissioned drawings from several experts for the house he'd purchased next door, ultimately it was Jamie's sketches which inspired him to say (always through an intermediary), "I want every one of these."

Home again, Jamie told us, "You can't move from one room in Musk's house to another without identifying yourself on each door with your fingerprints."

I said, "Really?" and Rob said, "That would make it pretty slow going." Jamie grinned. "Everything about him is kind of mysterious."

As IT DEVELOPED, JAMIE'S CAL POLY PROVIDED HER WITH MORE than an education. Only after several years away from school (and the end of another relationship), did she begin dating Mike Toole, who had graduated with a major in microbiology. The two found they had numerous attitudes in common—a love of sports, particularly tennis, and a calm approach to hard work and life's minor setbacks.

After three years of dating, one day when Jamie was elsewhere, Mike confided his plans—to several of us seated around Tracy's table. "There's this bridge near a major hotel. I'm asking some friends to hide nearby with video cameras. I'll propose to her on the bridge." Smiling, he held up a small box. "I've already got the ring."

Later we saw the video—which proved that Jamie was both surprised and thrilled.

Some time later, in advance of the wedding, they moved into an ideal Tustin condo, whose park-like environs included a nearby tennis court.

JUST AS JAMIE AND MIKE SEEMED SETTLED INTO A NEIGHBORHOOD and their two jobs, Tracy was once more struck by tragedy. This time it was Brad who, one night, seemed to have suffered a stroke. Suddenly, to Tracy's chagrin, he seemed fuzzy, unable to remember any details about his life—including whatever was the current year. (They'd now been married nine years.)

Tracy called us, and Rob and I rushed to her home. By then Brad had recovered somewhat and declared he was fine and didn't need medical help. The rest of us weren't convinced, and called Chris, who urged Tracy to take Brad to the St. Joseph hospital emergency room.

There Tracy ran into a bureaucratic buzz saw. The clerk at the desk told her to have Brad sit nearby while she filled out papers. "But he's had a stroke," she cried. "Shouldn't you take him back into a bed?"

"Just have him sit there," the woman insisted. "You need to fill out these papers."

"He needs immediate care," Tracy said. "Put him in a wheelchair, at least."

But the clerk paid no attention. In despair, Tracy began filling out the paperwork.

She'd hardly started when Brad suddenly fell forward out of the chair and onto his face. His nose, dripping blood, created a puddle which slowly crept across the floor.

The waiting room erupted into small shrieks from other patients. Suddenly an orderly came and scooped Brad up and into a wheelchair. Another arrived with rags to clean up the blood. Quickly, Brad was wheeled into the back and into a bed. Whereupon Tracy called us—and Rob and I hurried to the hospital.

Strange as it seemed, no diagnosis was found that night. Brad seemed to recover, and several days later he left on a business trip to Boston.

But Chris was concerned that something dire was going on. It was early Friday when Chris called Tracy. "Brad needs to come home right away—at the latest, by afternoon today—for an MRI."

"He doesn't want to," Tracy said. "He's planning to get here tomorrow, on Saturday,"

"Saturday's not good enough. You'll have to talk him into it," said Chris. "Tell him I said he's got to return before closing time on Friday. He can't wait for the weekend. MRI's aren't available then, except for emergencies."

Tracy conveyed Chris's message and somehow persuaded Brad to take a midday Friday plane—a schedule that would get him home while MRIs were still being offered at St. Joseph.

Arriving just at the crucial hour, he let Tracy whisk him away to the hospital.

Meanwhile, since we'd been invited to dinner at Mike and Jamie's, Rob and I—and soon Chris and Betty-Jo— gathered at their condo, waiting for Tracy and Brad to return.

When the time came, Brad was slow getting out of the car and Tracy was momentarily alone. She entered the condo white-faced, with tears in her eyes. We stared at her, all of us breathless.

"I need to tell you this before he comes in. He's got a brain tumor. It's called Glioblastoma." Chris understood, but the rest of us didn't. "It's a death sentence," she said. "With surgery, he may live awhile. Maybe a year. But ultimately it's fatal."

As one, we moaned, "Oh, no," and separately most of us began to cry. With all thoughts of dinner vanished, her news struck the family like a thunderclap. For the second time in her life, Tracy was facing the loss of a husband to cancer.

Even then, we didn't know how difficult the year would really be.

Chapter Thirty-One

A Second Goodbye

With the diagnosis from hell hanging over him, Brad went into surgery almost immediately. "I'll beat this," he said to Tracy and the doctor as he was being prepped, "I'll come out of it okay," and even his surgeon didn't disagree with him.

Privately, the doctor told Tracy, "With surgery we can give him an extra year."

"And even more?" she asked.

"Perhaps," he said. "But most of it, at least for the first half, will be a good year."

"We have to do it," she said. "My daughter's getting married early next year. We all want him there."

He nodded. "I think that's possible."

And so, early on a Tuesday in October, the team began. Using an enlarged computer screen, the neurosurgeon kept stopping his work, because each step, each cut, had to be viewed—an attempt to separate good brain matter from bad. How well he knew that both types of tissue looked the same. The process was painstaking and slow.

Eleven hours later, long after I'd gone home, Tracy's closest friends still remained with her in the hospital's waiting room. When the surgeon finally emerged, weary beyond description, Tracy and her friends all clapped.

EVEN AS BRAD RECOVERED, PLANS FOR JAMIE'S WEDDING BEGAN, NOW set for March 1. A good friend offered to let them use his several groomed acres for the ceremony. By late in the year, Brad became a willing participant.

Like all of today's weddings, the planning took months. But suddenly, just one week out, a major rainstorm was predicted for the area. The generous host knew the outdoor ceremony would no longer work. "When my tennis court gets flooded," he said, "there's no way to dry it out. And the surrounding areas will also be full of puddles. I feel terrible—but there's no way we can pull this off."

On the Monday before the Saturday wedding, Tracy consulted Mike and Jamie, who insisted the outdoor venue would be fine. "We'll make it work, Mom," said Jamie.

"In pouring rain?" Tracy asked. "With the tennis court flooded and your guests all getting sopping wet? For once the weather bureau isn't equivocal. There's no chance, they say, of decent weather this Saturday."

Over the objections of the wedding pair, Tracy was dealt an incredible stroke of good luck. The nearby tennis club where she'd learned to play the game, was miraculously available. With friends and family pitching in to make phone calls—to the caterer, flower providers, band, and guests—the message went out immediately, until all were aware of the new setting.

And sure enough, later in the week the downpour began, right on schedule. The generous man who'd offered his outdoor acreage had predicted correctly that it would have been a disaster.

And yet, as though the tennis club venue had been chosen from the beginning, Jamie and Mike were married under nearly perfect circumstances. Brad was well enough to walk Jamie down the abbreviated "aisle" and even make a short speech. Tracy's thirteen-year-old neighbor, a budding singer who was nearly professional, performed Andrew Lloyd Weber's "Love Changes Everything."

So Jamie had her ideal wedding after all. At age 27, she reveled in the kudos of her friends and family, who all considered her wedding to be outstanding ... and yes, marvelously romantic.

As is our family tradition, Rob and I, plus Tracy and Brad, and also Mike Toole's parents, accompanied the bridal pair on a Caribbean cruise. The journey was mostly good except for one moment when Tracy realized Brad had put their valuables in the suite's safe—and now couldn't remember the code. With no back-up access, the ship's mechanic had to tear it apart to retrieve their money.

THE REST OF THE YEAR BECAME A SAD, DOWNHILL SLIDE, WITH BRAD, whose optic nerve had been damaged by the surgery, unable to see clearly and becoming ever weaker and less able to work. For months, Tracy, and sometimes Dane, took him for daily appointments to an eye doctor for visual therapy. And briefly I tried to combat his failing eyesight with the use of flash cards ... though we could all tell our efforts were futile.

With his driver's license revoked, Brad one day got behind the wheel of his car, insisting, "I can drive." But within moments he smashed his Acura into the side of the garage. With that, he accepted the inevitable and gave up.

Brad was nothing, if not highly intelligent. Rob and I missed his participation in word games like Boggle, where, even as a newcomer, he invariably used clever adaptations and sometimes beat the lot of us, including my word-smith husband.

Late in the year, shots of steroids reduced the swelling in his brain but made him so combative the family had difficulty coping with his moods.

For Tracy it was another six months of hell. Toward the end her days were brightened, somewhat, by visits from friends, who invariably brought casseroles, and sometimes whole meals. And Rob was successful in persuading Brad to sign a will, bequeathing his video company to Tracy.

Later Tracy shared some of his assets, including his Acura, with his sisters, though she never confided an amount. Rob and I could only judge by their gratitude she must have been as generous as Brad would have hoped.

Eventually hospice stepped in, providing medications and sponge baths.

Since Brad could no longer climb stairs, Tracy moved his hospital bed to the family room.

I remember one poignant moment when Tracy cut herself with a kitchen knife. Brad noted her cry of pain, and from his bed, where he could see her at the sink, he called out (as though wishing he could help), "Sorry. Sorry."

Almost exactly one year from his diagnosis, Brad was on the verge of dying. Aware that he couldn't last the day, Tracy called on one of Brad's interns who played the guitar. "Please come sing to him," she said. And so, for about five hours, Anthony sang all the pieces Brad loved, accompanying himself as he sang.

Sitting quietly nearby, Rob and I and Jamie and Dane and Tracy listened to the music and waited through the hours until Brad took his last breath.

Months later, deciding that the best jobs went to people with advanced degrees, Jamie's Mike, who'd been running a small clock company, decided he needed to get his MBA. After much research, it seemed to him that the quickest route was to enter the Asade school in Barcelona. With that, he took out student loans and he and Jamie moved to Spain.

During the next year and a half, while Mike studied, Jamie did her own studying, preparing for the four-part exam that would make her a licensed landscape architect, able to sign off on complicated plans. Among other requirements, applicants had to qualify to design hard-scape, such as walls, patios, and pools, which meant memorizing numerous elements required for a structural engineer.

By the time Mike received his MBA, Jamie had returned several times to Santa Ana, then New York, where she finally passed the last of the required national exams—only to receive a new shock. The State of California required the passage of a separate, punishing exam. For this one, the applicant was required to memorize relevant (and irrelevant) information about a thousand different plants—including their Latin names.

188

"I can't do it," Jamie said. "It's too much. They've made it impossible. Who can remember both the English and Latin names for a thousand different plants? Not to mention the ideal conditions for their growth?" She was almost in tears. "I thought I was finished."

But being Jamie, she soon pulled herself together, and spent several additional months on tedious memorization. Back once more in California, she passed the nastiest of all the exams—and is now qualified to sign any and all landscape plans that she designs.

At last crowned with an MBA, Mike Toole spent a few months, still in Barcelona, applying to numerous corporations for a job. "If he doesn't find something soon," Jamie said, "we'll come back to America."

Just as they began to plan seriously for their return, Mike found an excellent position with Adidas—in Amsterdam.

To my dismay and Tracy's, they have no immediate plans to return.

For Rob and me, life has always been full of ironies. The moments you expect will be seamless and positive sometimes turn into failures. But more often, when we look ahead to a projected calamity we discover that out of it came a blessing we never expected.

Such was the irony—the amazing surprise—that awaited us long after Brad was gone.

CHAPTER THIRTY-TWO

Bravo, Match. Paul

TRACY IS PROBABLY THE MOST PRO-ACTIVE PERSON I KNOW. REFUSING to *stay down* over misfortunes, even tragedies, she invariably reacts in ways that serve her well.

After too many months of what was now a second widowhood, she confided to me, "I'm not going to spend the rest of my life alone."

With that, she signed up for Match.com. As I looked over her shoulder, both literally and figuratively, I could tell that the dating site was cleverly designed with, among other useful features, an impenetrable firewall. Participants' phone numbers, email contacts, and home addresses were never revealed. Before two people arranged to meet (usually at a public site for coffee), each of them could read the self-reported bios and view the photos of potential acquaintances.

I found it fascinating how much the pictures themselves revealed—whether the man thought his muscles were his best feature, or he was devoted to his motorcycle, or whether he was willing to reveal that he'd been married and now had young children.

After a while, Tracy entered some professionally-taken photos ... none designed to be sexually provocative, but only to reveal her in a variety of different settings.

She received numerous responses from an assortment of interesting, clearly eligible males. Among those she met for coffee were several who seemed possible. Yet one highly-placed businessman whom she agreed to join for dinner at an upscale restaurant was intent on immediately bending

191

her to his will … among other subtle messages, he gave her an unasked for shoulder message.

Tracy knew enough to look for the small signs—including from fellows who seemed to be hiding information, such as where they lived or worked … or even, rarely, whether they were still married. Some were careless enough to make incriminating comments. One doctor said, "My office manager just got sick. I told my staff, 'Get rid of her.'"

It was a captivating process for anyone like me, always intrigued by how humans behave.

Eventually one of her coffee dates led to Paul Richard.

FOR THREE YEARS, ROB AND I HAVE FOUND IT A BEGUILING STORY— how the Paul encounter developed.

Paul was unlike everyone else. Calm, thoughtful, and self-assured at their first coffee date, he didn't try to overwhelm her; instead the two found they could talk casually, as though they'd just met on a plane.

A graduate of the University of Rhode Island, he worked for the Orange County school district—a county-wide responsibility for which he is a technology coordinator. In addition, he teaches an online technology class.

Tracy soon learned he'd raised two daughters by himself, and that the young women, both college graduates, were about the same ages as her own two kids.

He was tall and trim. Like Tracy, he enjoyed being physically active, and in fact he belonged to a hiking club. On one occasion when she was with him on a hike, Tracy noticed that when one of the female members couldn't keep up, it was Paul who hung back to encourage her.

Soon they were dating exclusively—which was when Rob and I became acquainted. Within months we learned that he had skills which weren't immediately obvious. Like Chris, who never brags about what he can do, it seemed Paul could fix anything.

Before long, he installed guiding lights along our front walkway, and an automatic light-up system for the back door—jobs Rob and I didn't ask for, but which Paul thought were necessary, so he just did them.

For the three years we've known him, this is typical. He does so many repairs for his family and ours that he now says with a smile, "If I miss a few days going to Home Depot, they call me up, asking where I've been."

Even Tracy's small black and white dog, Ollie, has taken on a new allegiance. Every night around eight, Tracy's movie dog (who attracts wonder and delight wherever he goes), trots over to Paul and looks up into his hero's face with an eager expression. He might as well be saying, "It's time for our evening walk." And while patient, the animal doesn't waver, but follows Paul around, still gazing at his master with quiet longing. At which the dog-whisperer, to the tune of a couple of excited barks, slips on Ollie's small harness, and out they go, into the dark neighborhood.

Although Tracy is predictably generous, Rob and I have noticed what happens after dinner at their house: invariably it's Paul who says, "I've wrapped up a couple of pieces of chicken for you to take home."

All of which reminds us of the relationship Tracy enjoyed so long ago with her first husband, Geoff. As before, it's Tracy whose hearty laugh and bright interest in everyone around her keeps her in the spotlight. Yet now it's Paul who's right there, quietly stepping in to barbecue steaks … and afterwards unobtrusively loading the dishwasher.

It's no surprise to any of us that he's become an integral part of our family.

Rob sums it up best: "I've been watching him for three years, and I know there must be a flaw or two, but so far I haven't found any."

Chapter Thirty-Three

A Long Life's Big Reward

Unless you were married at some ridiculous age, like nineteen (as I was), it's unlikely you'll ever get to know your great grandchildren. Actually, it takes more than one generation of hot-blooded early marriers and conceivers to accomplish this feat. In fact, such a result also requires that the original couple stay healthy for longer than statistics suggest.

So far, Rob and I and our oldest kids fit every category. Meaning we're well-acquainted with some fascinating great grandchildren ... "a flock," Rob says, which currently numbers fourteen.

To tell the truth, three of the oldest girls inquire on a regular basis, "When are you going to write about me?"

Though I'm not at all sure what lifetime goal Nora, now 10 and one of the three, has in mind, we've already seen strong leanings from Christy's twin daughters—Marley, 12, who yearns to be a writer, and her twin, Malena.

As we adults have observed, Marley can't stop reading. Even in the face of high activity in Chris's backyard pool, when kids her age are whooping, giggling, and sailing down the water-fed slide, Marley is apt to be somewhere off by herself, completely absorbed in a book. In fact, books have been such a long-standing part of Marley's life, that at age seven she wrote a letter to two authors—a worshipful piece that her mother, Christy, just happened to find near the front door of their apartment. (I've carefully preserved it all these years). Here, in her 2nd grade handwriting, is what she wrote:

to: Stan and Jan Berenstein. I love your books. I am 7!! Your books make me happy wen I am sad. I wrily want Santa Bear *and* Too Much Birthday *and* Moving Day. *My name is Marley!! I love* Trouble with Friends *and* Messy Room. *I thenk* Get Stay Fright *and* Too Much TV *are fany. I still like the rest!! you are the best!! Kan you gise get me* Moving Day *and* Santa Bear, *and* Too Much Birthday? *Love, Marley*

How lucky for all of us that Christy happened to find that letter!

Marley's twin, Malena, is much more likely to relate to the world around her, but especially to Christy, her mother. Christy says, "She knows what's going on and who is doing what at all times. She often divines what I am going to say before I speak, and if asked, can usually report what I'm thinking. It's uncanny. When she was three, I walked out to go to work in my typical black suit with a new, but unremarkable blouse. (Christy is a deputy public defender.) As I walked past her bedroom she called out, "Mommy, where did you get that shirt?"

"I was stunned that (1) she had such a detailed mental inventory of my clothes that she recognized it was new and (2) that in the split second I walked past her bedroom she noticed it.

"If anything is missing in the house, Malena can find it.

"She is also one of my best helpers. Though she likes to complain that we 'treat her like a slave,' it is only because any project we are working on becomes ten times easier with her around. She will fetch things and seems to know what you need before you ask. My dad (Chris) commented on this when she was helping him in the garage.

"She is also the kid who can jump into any social situation and make friends—which she's proved on play dates and summer camp. Our British friends joke that they are going to steal her to make her their 4th child."

When Marley and Malena come down from Berkeley to visit their grandparents, Chris and Betty-Jo, Malena always relates to Nora, who, though two years younger but just as tall, is apt to consider herself in charge of every child within shouting distance. And some adults as well.

With Nora, Kelly and Matt's child, this is not a new phenomenon. Most of us can remember this little girl as she reacted to the party after her

Aunt Lauren and Dan's wedding. She was about two, then, and busy dancing on the outdoor stage. Unlike most kids her age, her movements involved
her arms, hips, shoulders, hands, and facial expressions. She took up her
position near the band, and each time the music paused, even momentarily,
Nora hurried over to the leader and said, "Play another one."

Her command was not lost on the musicians. Long past her bedtime,
Nora made frequent trips to the edge of the stage, inciting the players to
keep going. Nora never stopped dancing as long as there was music to
accompany her.

My next memory of Nora came indirectly, from Tracy, when the tot
was about three and a half. It happened that Nora stayed overnight, with
Tracy as her baby sitter.

Next morning, Tracy was still upstairs and Nora was down, when the
front door opened—with the weekly housekeeper using her key. Surprised,
and with hands on hips, Nora immediately confronted her. "Who are you?"
she asked the woman, "and what are you doing here?"

Berry laughed. "I came to clean the house."

Nora stood her ground. "You don't need to clean this house. This
house is already clean."

In disbelief about what she was hearing, Berry tried to explain. "Tracy's
expecting me," she said. "She'd want me to stay."

In the face of this refusal, Nora said, "You need to go upstairs and
talk to Tracy."

When Berry didn't seem inclined to follow Nora's orders, the girl ran
upstairs herself to inform Tracy about the situation below.

Later, the housekeeper told Tracy the whole story—and couldn't stop
laughing.

FOR SOME TIME, NORA'S OLDER BROTHER, OLIVER, THEN FIVE, HAD
been reciting the continents and states to anyone who would listen. His
memory was uncanny—and he quickly noticed we adults were both pleased
and amused.

Before Nora turned four, it happened that Tracy and her friend, Pam, took Nora and Oliver out to Irvine Park, where Nora's mother, Kelly, was riding in a bicycle race.

On the way, Oliver was, as usual, regaling everyone in the car by reciting what he knew—first, listing the continents of the world, then naming the various states within the U.S. Both Tracy and Pam were impressed.

Shortly after they arrived at the park, Nora had to go to the bathroom. Without informing the adults, she simply took off, running across an open area to reach the toilets.

Pam ran after her, and so did Oliver. As Pam caught up with Nora, Pam began scolding the three-year-old for running off into a crowd. "It's dangerous," she said. "You can't just take off like that. You have to tell us first." She would have gone on, except for what Nora did next.

Impatient, Nora listened to just so much of Pam's spiel. And then she turned to her brother. "Oliver," she said, "talk to her about the states."

Pam later said, "She couldn't have been clearer. She might as well have said, 'Get that woman off my back!'"

In 2011, when Nora was still about four, Rob and I took Kelly's kids out for supper at the local Tustin brewery, where we picked a table outside. The girl who came to wait on us was young, with her hair in today's usual straight, hang-down style.

After our first course, the girl returned. Nobody else noticed that there'd been a change—but Nora did. She said, "You put your hair up." And sure enough, the waitress's locks were now in a pony tail.

As he's grown, now a young lad of 12, Nora's brother, Oliver, is different from her in every way. Around the family, he is as happy as the other youngsters cavorting in Chris's and Betty-Jo's pool, but he's less apt to interact with the other kids, and more likely to come by and talk to the adults.

Warm with us and invariably smiling, Oliver is basically a student. He is absorbed by facts on every subject, and retains what he reads.

On a recent Christmas, his family gave him a large black cowboy hat—it was felt and what I'd call sophisticated—and to our surprise he wore it often. This was the kind of headpiece a cowboy might don when he was dressed up and taking a cowgirl to town. Yet this fancy dude hat suited Oliver perfectly.

Last year at Christmas, Rob gave Oliver a fat, illustrated science book, which I imagined he would find dull. Not so. Since Christy's kids had come down for the holidays, I soon saw Oliver and Marley stretched out on the living room floor together, totally absorbed in Oliver's book. They were as engaged as most kids might be with a cell-phone movie.

Oliver has already declared that he'd like to be a marine scientist when he grows up. Judging by his long-standing fascination with geography, even the geographical placement of foreign nations, we wouldn't be at all surprised if Oliver ends up a professor.

THESE THEN, ARE THE GREAT-GRANDCHILDREN WE SEE MOST OFTEN, either because they live in our area, or because they're the oldest, and most likely to come to down from Berkeley for visits with their professional grandmother, Betty-Jo, and her partner in kid entertainment—jokester and pilot, Chris.

Yet right behind them is a second group of younger kids, whom we find equally engaging when they're nearby.

So far they've generated fewer stories, but those we have are delicious.

CHAPTER THIRTY-FOUR

Five Pixies at a Distance

AMONG THE GREAT GRANDKIDS WE DON'T SEE OFTEN ARE GEOFF AND Amber's two, Ella and Emmett, who live so close to the top edge of the state, they're on the verge of tipping right out of California and into Oregon.

From Berkeley north to Eureka it's a long drive, with airplane service so scant and expensive, it's not worth flying. Though Rob and I have made the drive a few times, we've become ever less enthusiastic about long trips by car.

On the rare occasions when we've seen Ella, Rob was apt to tease her and call her "Emma." Each time, even when she was only three, Ella objected vigorously, saying "I'm Ella!"

On one occasion, after Rob had once again teased her at the restaurant where we were having breakfast, Ella soon left with her father. On the way out, she turned to Geoff and said about Rob, "He can be irritating, can't he?"

As of this writing, August of 2018, Ella is now seven and Emmett is four. We hear from Chris and Betty-Jo that the family is thriving.

LAUREN, CHRIS AND BETTY-JO'S THIRD GIRL, HAS SETTLED IN SOUTH Lake Tahoe with husband Dan, where Lauren is an RN, and Dan runs a restaurant. Still, their most noteworthy achievement might be that they've created a clone. Young Annalise, at 3 ½, looks so much like her mother that viewing them side by side is like looking at the same person at two different ages. (The same likeness holds for Rob as a baby.)

At the moment, young Corbin, five, has his dad's grin, albeit with undertones of mischief. And indeed, one morning a couple of years ago the two youngsters managed to pull off a caper which their parents would have thought impossible.

Corbin was then 3 and Annalise only 2, though between them they created an event their parents will never forget.

Here is the account, as written by their father, Dan:

As I lay next to my wife in the comfort of my king-sized bed, I am awakened by the discomfort of a deafening silence. I glance at the bedside clock: it reads 7:15 a.m., and in our house waking up this late is uncommon. With a sense of urgency, and knowing that my two-year-old daughter is too innocent to tell anything but the truth, I yell down to her, "Annalise, what are you guys doing?"

With a clumsy thump, thump, thump, I hear her miniature feet barreling across the hardwood floor. I can tell she is heading from garage through kitchen, around the corner, through living room, and finally halting at the foot of the staircase. With a mischievous tone, she calmly yells up the stairway, "Corbin is painting."

"Corbin is painting?" I repeat. *Oh, shit.*

As quickly as I can, I shoot out of bed. In my white cotton socks I slide around the corner and run down the stairs like a gazelle—a gazelle chased by a cheetah. The minute I reach the hardwood floor at the bottom, the scent of fresh paint hits me in the nose.

Remember, I just mentioned those miniature feet thumping across the hardwood floor? Well, I follow green and white footprints all the way back … from the stairs, through the living room, past the fireplace, through the kitchen and right to the garage.

As I enter the garage, the scent of fresh paint grows stronger, and with the glow of the florescent garage lights, I see for the first time a plethora of colors with which my children have doused the entire space.

The door to the refrigerator is wide open, with tags of black spray paint inside and out. The door to the outside shed has been used like a Bob Ross canvas from the 80s. Even the washer and dryer have those same miniature footprints stamped across the top. Nearby, my son's bike is also covered in paint, blended into all the rest like camouflage.

I immediately decide there is no way that two very young children could do this kind of damage. I must be looking at the work of vandals.

But there in the middle of that cold, well-lit garage, stand my two, paint-speckled offspring holding cans of spray paint and paint brushes. Next to them, on what used to be a black, foam-tiled floor, is a gallon can of green house paint, and also various cans of spray paint—plus the paint-covered butter knife used to open the can.

Most startling of all, I finally realize how the kids accomplished this. All our paint has been kept on a high shelf at least eight feet above the cement. With a stepstool pulled against the Whirlpool washing machine, it becomes clear that Corbin has climbed onto the washer, and from there was able to pull down, and perhaps hand to Annalise, the various containers of paint.

I'm thinking, *Where do I start?*

The answer is, *With the kids, of course.*

After stripping off both children's paint-soaked pajamas, I swiftly scoop up my son and head for the shower, telling my daughter, "Wait there, Annalise. And don't touch anything."

As the colorful soap water runs down Corbin's body into the tub and down the drain, I can't help but think how white and clean this tub once was, and how it now looks like it's host to a fresh puddle of mud on a rainy fall morning.

Following the prison-style hose down and scrub of child number one, came the same unwilling cleanse of the second culprit. Doing the best I can to rid their young, sensitive skin of paint, I dry them with a clean, soft towel and sit them down on the leather sofa in the living room—which at that point doubles as their courtroom.

Before starting the lecture I'm about to give them, and before explaining to them that what they did was wrong, I reflect back on the 20 minutes of chaos that began my morning. From the eerie silence that awoke me, to the pitter patter of a clumsy child running across hardwood floors, to the graffiti-covered garage, to the watered-down paint draining from the tub, I realize this won't be the last time something like this happens.

Suddenly, strangely, I'm completely happy with this; these are my kids, and this is my family, and I love them with all my heart.

CURRENTLY, THE REST OF OUR 14 GREAT-GRANDCHILDREN ARE ALSO at such a distance that visits are both rare and special. Even Brandon and Rachel and their two, Scarlett and Spencer, are nearly an hour's drive away.

With Rob's aversion to freeway driving, we've been to their house only twice. On one occasion, the kids proudly showed off their bedrooms. As we were viewing five-year-old Spencer's very clean and well-organized room, he was busy using hands and feet to propel himself ever higher within the door frame. As he reached the top beam, he delivered a message down to Rob and me. "My bedroom," he said, "isn't usually this neat."

We adults all laughed, and I glanced at Rachel—her expression a cross between mild chagrin and laughter.

Clearly, Spencer was reflecting his parents' high regard for honesty.

Still, on the Fourth of July this year, we persuaded Brandon's family to make the trek to our area and share both dinner and fireworks. While neither Rachel nor Brandon offered any vignettes about their children, Rob and I could see that Scarlet and Spencer, ready to begin first and fourth grades, have become charming individuals … and as they've been in the past, will doubtless continue to be teachers' pets.

WITH THREE FAMILIES LIVING IN VARIOUS DISTANT PARTS OF OUR state, it's understandable that the farthest away, Geoff and Amber, rarely venture to Southern California, meaning Rob and I have missed substantial portions of their kids' early childhoods.

The truth is, we're more apt to see Erica and Christian's boy and girl in Virginia—whom I've described in earlier chapters. They now have a second baby girl. Rob and I hope to meet her soon.

Now that Tracy's Jamie and Mike Toole have a new baby girl, born in Amsterdam in April, 2018, Rob and I have already made stops there on our way to and from a cruise.

As an unusual side note, Tracy treated us to photos of Jamie playing active tennis in her ninth month of pregnancy … and stranger still, she reported that her daughter, in that last month (and to us, unwisely), ventured out on her bicycle. And yes, in Amsterdam's thick bicycle traffic.

As it turns out, baby Eva was equally busy in that same pre-natal period quietly growing hair. When she arrived a week late, she had such a full supply of dark, shiny locks that only a head band would keep them under control. Within a short time, Jamie found herself entertaining her infant by bathing her, then blow-drying the baby's hair.

With all the ten families so scattered, geographically, it takes intense planning from Rob, and a designated, exotic family vacation site, like the Virgin Islands or Hawaii, to bring them all together—and even then we never seem to get everyone.

I suspect arranging the meeting of the United Nations General Assembly might be easier. At least the various countries can assign the logistics to someone with authority and plenty of available time.

Four Generations of the Wills Clan in the British Virgin Islands.

CHAPTER THIRTY-FIVE

Why We're Hanging On

As I declared in the opening pages how, since age ten, I've spent an undue amount of energy maintaining my hold on earth, I am now, at 89, clinging to that position tighter than ever. As much as possible I avoid foods with a bad reputation, like high fructose corn syrup ... and I've made short daily walks part of my routine—though I can't claim to enjoy them, only that I relish "having done them."

For several decades now, I've demonstrated to my grandkids that I can still do the "plank" ... which is a floor exercise in which your whole body is suspended in space solely by arms and legs. Their astonishment is one reason this remains a permanent feature of my floor routine. Because hey, nothing is more fun than amazing your grandkids.

What I haven't shared with them is how time seems to speed up as you get older—how the weeks gallop by so fast, that when you get out a week's worth of tea bags, they're gone in four days.

Another unshared thought is about my continuing tenacity for remaining where I am—though the kids may have guessed it. What they don't know is how, over the years, the reasons have changed. I am now determined to witness a return to the America we all once knew: a United States led by a president who is at once just and compassionate, honest, highly-intelligent, and an experienced leader—complemented by an equally qualified Congress.

To this end both Rob and I write blogs and essays, comparing what we have now to a hoped-for resurgence of good old Lincolnesque values, both fiscally and ethically.

The truth is, I care too much to easily relinquish my spot on earth. I'm staying right in this house as long as I'm able to write, to warn, and in some small way to rally like-minded voters. Our country needs me and Rob, and everyone like us, to fight back until our leaky craft stops sinking.

Our ever-growing family needs us, too.

And anyway, we're so engrossed in the unfurling stories of grandkids and great grandkids, they've become like characters in a novel, too intriguing to stop caring about.

Which are logical reasons for both of us to stick around for as long as possible.

THE END

MARALYS WILLS HAS LIVED THREE DISTINCT LIVES: AUTHOR OF fifteen published books, teacher of college students, and mother of six children—five boys and a girl.

Educated at Stanford and UCLA, she is married to a retired trial attorney. She currently teaches novel writing on the college level, and in 2000 was named Teacher of the Year.

Her most challenging project, a poignant memoir titled *Higher Than Eagles,* became her biggest triumph, garnering excellent reviews and five movie options.

Wills considers public speaking the dessert for all the hard work of writing, and relishes every moment spent with a receptive audience. She welcomes readers' input.

Contact her: Maralys@Cox.net or www.Maralys.com

Word of mouth is crucial for any author to succeed. If you enjoyed the book, please consider leaving a review on Amazon, even if it's only a line or two; it will make all the difference and is very much appreciated

www.ingramcontent.com/pod-product-compliance
Lightning Source LLC
Chambersburg PA
CBHW072345090426
42741CB00012B/2924